THE SOUL WHISPERS

Angie Real

Dedication

Remember this: in every moment, you hold the power of choice. You can stay trapped in victimhood or rise as your hero. The key lies in understanding why we sometimes feel powerless and then boldly overcoming it. It's about breaking free from the chains of victim mentality, taking responsibility, and forging a new path forward. If you have children, lead by example.

Break open the superhero cape and show them what true strength looks like: fighting for yourself, for them, and for a better tomorrow. Be honest with yourself, for while you cannot control how others make you feel, you hold the ultimate power over how you respond. This is your journey, your fight, and your victory.

The question is: *Are you ready to choose to be the hero of your own story?*

Through my life's journey, I've discovered a powerful truth: Be the mentor you wish you had. Embrace trust in God's plan and let go of worries. My guiding motto is "Que sera, sera" – whatever will be, will be. Living with this faith has transformed my life, filling it with peace, hope, and purpose.

~Tanya Graham

This is a heartfelt tribute to my incredible friend and warrior - Tanya Graham. Her words reflect the depth of her spirit, and her presence leaves a lasting light in every life she touches.

Author's Note

I'm here with you. Maybe we've never met, but I know the weight you're carrying—the ache in your chest, the exhaustion that seeps into your bones, the way the world feels unfamiliar now. I know what it's like to move through your days pretending you're fine, while inside, you're just trying to keep from falling apart.

You don't have to explain it to me—I feel it with you. That heavy silence. That questioning of everything. That mix of anger, grief, and disbelief that can crash into you without warning. You're not crazy. You're not broken. You're human, and you're surviving something that would shake anyone to their core.

I want you to know this: you're not alone in it. I'm right here, holding space for the messy, the raw, and the unspoken. You don't have to rush your healing or prove your strength. You get to take up space in your pain and your process, and I'll be here—reminding you that you are seen, you are held, and you are not walking this road by yourself.

Contents

Introduction

There are nights when the pain feels utterly unbearable. Nights when you stare at the ceiling and wonder how you're still breathing with a heart that feels so shattered. Nights when you ask yourself if you will ever wake up from this nightmare or if this is just how life will feel from now on – forever raw, forever broken.

I know, because I have lived those nights too. I have been the woman sitting on the cold floor, holding the broken pieces of a love I thought would last forever, wondering how I became the one who wasn't *"enough"* to be chosen, to be protected, to be loved completely and faithfully.

I have screamed into the darkness. I have begged God, the Universe, the heavens, anyone who would listen, to take away the pain, to make it make sense, to give me back the life I thought was mine.

And yet, here I am. Not because I found some secret shortcut. Not because I am stronger or better or wiser. But because somehow, even in the darkest hours, there was a tiny, flickering light inside me that refused to go out. There is a light inside you too—small, stubborn, holy.

If you are holding this book right now, know this: You are not alone. You are not broken beyond hope. You are not invisible to the Divine. You are not worthless. You are a woman who loved deeply. You are a woman who gave her heart with hope and trust.

And none of this, none of this betrayal, this devastation, this heartbreak… is a reflection of your worth. Betrayal says nothing about how lovable you are. It speaks only to how broken and cowardly the other person is. You are still worthy. Still radiant. Still holy in your tenderness. You are standing at a sacred crossroads. Maybe you're wondering if you should stay and try to rebuild.

Maybe you're wondering if you should gather every last shred of your courage and walk away. Maybe you are too numb to know anything except that you can't live one more day in this agony.

Wherever you are right now, it's okay. You do not have to have all the answers today. You do not have to *"be strong"* every moment. You do not have to pretend you are okay. You only have to promise yourself this: **I will not abandon myself. Not for anyone, not ever again.**

In the pages ahead, we will walk this journey together. I will not give you false hope. I will not give you easy platitudes. I will provide you with truth, tools, and the fierce love of a woman who has stood in the wreckage and chosen to rise anyway.

Your healing will not be linear. There will be days you feel powerful, and days you can barely breathe. Both are sacred. Both are part of becoming.

You are not broken beyond repair. You are broken open so that you can rebuild a life even more true, more beautiful, more fearlessly yours than the one you thought you lost.

You are still here. You are still worthy. You are still becoming.

Chapter 01:

The Nature of Betrayal

When the World Keeps Spinning, and You're Shattered

Betrayal doesn't just break your heart. It breaks you. It splits your soul wide open in the most intimate, brutal way, like someone reaching into your chest and ripping out the one thing you thought was safe. And the worst part? The world keeps spinning. People keep talking. Life keeps moving, while you're standing still, shattered into a thousand invisible pieces.

Betrayal isn't a single moment. It's a slow bleed. It's the 2 a.m. sob you choke on so you don't wake the kids. It's the smile you fake at the grocery store while dying inside. It's the replay reel in your head that never, ever stops.

No one tells you that betrayal feels like death, except you don't get a funeral, a eulogy, or flowers. There's no collective mourning. No *"I'm so sorry for your loss."* Just the hollow ache of silence where your love used to live.

And maybe the worst part? You begin to question everything. Not just them, but you. Was it all a lie? Was I blind? Was I not enough to be chosen, to be protected?

You don't just grieve the person who broke your trust. You grieve the woman you were before the lie. The one who believed love meant safety—the one who held onto loyalty like a sacred vow.

The one who believed that if she gave enough, loved hard enough, sacrificed deeply enough… it would be enough. You lose her, and no one sees the funeral in your eyes. This isn't just heartbreak. This is the unraveling of your identity. The shattering of your inner compass. The decimation of every *"truth"* you once clung to. And still, you wake up. You breathe. You move through another day with trembling legs and a smile that fools almost everyone.

Almost. Because underneath it all, there's a scream in your bones that never stops. You feel it in the quiet moments, in the stillness of night, when the mask falls and the ache rushes in like a flood. You question: *"Was I ever loved… or just convenient?" "Did he ever see me… or just what I could give him?" "How do I go on, knowing I was not chosen when it mattered most?"*

When the Ache Turns Inward

And then… the self-blame creeps in. Maybe if I was prettier. Less emotional. More adventurous. Less tired. More something. But listen to me right now, beautiful soul: This was never about your worth. This was about someone else's wounds. Their cowardice. Their inability to honor what was sacred.

You didn't fail. You loved. You opened your heart and built a home in someone who didn't know how to cherish it. That doesn't make you foolish. It makes you fierce. It makes you divine. It makes you real.

You are not crazy for falling apart. You are not being dramatic for needing space to breathe. You are not weak for feeling like the ground beneath you has disappeared. You are surviving the impossible and doing it without applause.

Every shaky breath you take is an act of defiance. Every tear you shed is a cleansing. Every moment you choose to keep living, even when it hurts like hell, that is power. You're still here. Bleeding. Bending. But not broken. Because you were never meant to stay in pieces.

Recognizing Betrayal Trauma Symptoms

This pain? It's not *"just heartbreak."* It's trauma: deep, visceral, soul-level trauma. Your nervous system isn't just sad, it's screaming. Because your body knows what your heart doesn't want to admit:

You were not safe. And when safety is ripped away by the very person you trusted most, your brain flips into survival mode. This isn't being sensitive. This is biology. Psychology. Truth.

You may be experiencing:

- **Hypervigilance:** Obsessively checking their location, analyzing texts, looking for lies behind every word.

- **Intrusive thoughts:** Replay of every red flag you ignored, every moment you now question.

- **Sleep disruption:** Either insomnia or the kind of exhaustion that pulls you under like a wave.

- **Panic attacks:** Sudden, crippling waves of fear that feel like you're dying

- **Physical pain:** Headaches, gut issues, a tight chest, trauma lives in the body.

- **Appetite swings:** Eating nothing or everything, trying to fill the emptiness or gain control.

- **Cognitive fog:** Forgetting simple tasks, feeling like your brain has short-circuited.

- **Disconnection:** Like you're watching yourself from the outside, numb and frozen.

- **Mistrust:** Of him, of others, even of yourself, especially your intuition.

Let's name it for what it is: Betrayal trauma is real. And you are not being *"dramatic."* You are responding appropriately to a violation of the deepest kind. Let that truth settle into your bones. You are not broken, you are wounded. And wounds are meant to be cared for, not ignored.

They require light. They require tending. They require someone to say, *"I see you. I believe you. I'm with you."* Let that someone be me. Let that someone be you.

Because this is where healing begins. Not in pretending. Not in bypassing. Not in *"just moving on."* Healing begins here, in this tender, trembling place where you admit: *"I was hurt. I didn't deserve it. And I am worth the effort to come back home to myself."*

You may not believe it yet, but I do. And if all you can do right now is keep breathing, then breathe! Because one day, not too far from now, those breaths will turn into a roar. And that roar will be the sound of you rising.

Closing Whispers

(For when the ache is too loud and the silence is even louder)

You didn't imagine it. You didn't overreact. You didn't deserve it. You were loyal to someone who confused love with possession. You handed your heart to someone who didn't know how to hold anything without cracking it open. And that wasn't your failure; it was their limitation.

There's no guidebook for this kind of pain. No manual for waking up in a life that feels like a crime scene. But here's what I need you to know: Even now, in the ache, you are sacred. You are still whole beneath the wreckage. You are still worthy of a love that holds, honors, and chooses you, without apology, without betrayal, without question.

Let this be your beginning, not your end. Not the closing of your story, but the first spark of your rising. You don't have to have it all figured out. You just have to stay. Stay with yourself. Stay with your truth. Stay with your breath, one inhale at a time, until it no longer feels like you're drowning in your ribs.

You are not lost. You are being reborn.

Soul Reflection

Questions to Sink Into

Where in my body do I carry the weight of betrayal right now? Describe it.

_____

_____

_____

_____

_____

_____

_____

_____

What truths have I been too afraid to acknowledge about my pain fully?

_____

_____

_____

_____

_____

_____

_____

What would it feel like to believe that this heartbreak is not the end of my story, but the beginning of a new one?

_____
_____
_____
_____
_____
_____
_____

What do I want my healing to look like, not for anyone else, but for my soul?

_____
_____
_____
_____
_____
_____
_____

Sacred Mantra

"Though my heart has shattered, my spirit still breathes.

Each breath is a sacred act of survival.

I am not broken, I am becoming."

Speak this aloud daily, morning and night, standing in front of a mirror.

Healing Ritual: The Candle of Survival

You will need:

- One white candle

- One journal

- A quiet space where you won't be disturbed

Instructions:

1. Light the white candle as the sun is setting.

2. Sit quietly in front of it, breathing slowly, feeling your chest rise and fall.

3. Whispers to yourself: *"I survived the day. I am still breathing. I honor my pain and my perseverance."*

4. Write one sentence in your journal: *"Today, despite everything, I stayed alive. That is enough."*

5. Blow out the candle with gratitude for your endurance.

Chapter 02:

Standing at the Crossroads: Salvage or Let Go

When the Silence Screams Louder Than the Betrayal

There comes a moment in every shattered marriage when the noise falls away and you are left standing alone, stripped bare, at the crossroads of your soul.

It does not feel courageous. It does not feel brave or strong or empowered. It feels like dying slowly, silently, without anyone noticing. It feels like the breath caught in your throat when you realize the person you trusted most was the one who burned your world down. It feels like clutching at the remains of a life you once believed was forever, while the cold, brutal truth gnashes at your ankles: It may never be the same again. And you may not survive it the way you thought you would.

You look down at your hands and wonder how they're still holding on. You wonder how your legs keep standing when your soul has crumpled to the floor. You wonder if it's even possible to go on living when the heart inside your chest has been fractured in so many places, it no longer beats the same.

The crossroads are not kind. They are not patient. They do not offer easy answers. They do not promise fairness, or redemption, or understanding from the ones who hurt you. They do not explain why you gave everything and still ended up here, standing in the middle of the wreckage with no map, no guide, no companion.

Here, the universe hands you a mirror, not a map. And it asks you: *"Who are you willing to become to save yourself?"* Not who you were before. Not the woman who kept the peace. Not the woman who bent herself in half trying to make it work. Not the woman who gave chance after chance, hoping this time would be different.

But the woman you were always meant to be, if you were willing to burn the illusions to the ground.

Two Roads, Both Lined with Fire

One path stretches out: Stay. Try again. Open the wound again and again, hoping this time the bleeding will stop. Hope he has changed. Hope you can forget. Hope you can be enough to make it different.

You will tell yourself, *"This time could be better."* You will search his eyes for signs of remorse. You will bargain with yourself, with the universe, with the ghost of the woman you used to be. You will wonder if maybe love is supposed to hurt this much. If maybe forgiveness means forgetting. If perhaps you were too sensitive, too demanding, too much.

The other path yawns wide and terrifying: Leave. Tear your own heart from the life you built. Start over alone. Face the nights with no comfort but your arms wrapped around your trembling body.

You will stare at the empty space in your bed and ache for the illusion of safety. You will question your strength. You will doubt your worth. You will grieve the dream with a cry that cracks your chest open.

Both roads will break you. Both roads will require your rebirth.

There is no gentle exit from betrayal. There is no path untouched by pain. You cannot unknow what you now know. You cannot unknow the weight of betrayal. You cannot unknow the way love can twist into something that wounds you while you beg for it to heal you. You will stand at this crossroads longer than you think. Longer than you want to. Longer than you're comfortable with. Long enough for others to grow tired of your indecision, while you fight the greatest war of your life behind quiet eyes and tired smiles.

You will try to trick yourself into believing there is a third path. one where none of this happened. One where he didn't lie, didn't cheat, didn't destroy the trust you so lovingly handed to him. You will ache for the version of him that existed only in your dreams. The one who protected you. Who saw you. Who chose you.

The one who never showed up in real life but lived vividly in the hope that made you stay. You will miss the man he could have been. Not the one who betrayed you, but the one who almost healed you. The one you saw glimpses of in the beginning. The one who said all the right things when he was trying not to lose you. The one who disappeared the moment things got hard.

The Sacred Rebuilding of a Worthy Woman

And in your loneliest hour, you will whisper to yourself: *"I deserved better. I always deserved better."* The words will feel foreign at first, like a language you forgot how to speak. But deep down, your soul knows it's the truth. This moment is sacred. This moment is where women are reborn. Not because they wanted to be. But because life asked them to choose themselves when everyone else abandoned them. Because they finally looked around at the ashes and said, *"I am not rebuilding for him. I am rebuilding for me."*

If you stay, you must build something new, not on lies, not on blind hope, but on truth, accountability, and fierce self-love. You cannot patch a crumbling house with apologies. You cannot sweep betrayal under the rug and call it resolved. You cannot smile through pain and call it forgiveness. You cannot be the only one doing the work and call it a partnership.

If you leave, you must grieve the death of your dream. You must let yourself mourn, not just the man, but the thought you were building together. The vacations were never taken. The anniversaries that will no longer be celebrated. The future that now belongs to someone else.

You must build a sanctuary from the ashes of your undoing. And that sanctuary won't be built overnight. It will rise slowly, in sacred layers: breath by breath, boundary by boundary, truth by truth.

Neither choice makes you weak. Neither choice makes you foolish.

You are already victorious. You stood in the fire and lived. You stood in the storm and did not disappear. You looked betrayal in the eye and said, *"You may have broken me, but I will not abandon myself again."* You survived the first betrayal. You are surviving the war within your own heart. And no matter what you choose, stay or go, you are allowed to demand a life that feels like love, not survival.

You are allowed to want peace. You are allowed to want joy. You are allowed to rebuild without shame or explanation. There is a whisper inside you, steady and ancient, that will not be silenced: *"I am worthy. I have always been worthy. Even here. Especially here."*

Even in the darkness. Even in doubt. Even in the messy, brutal middle of it all. You do not have to decide today. You do not have to rush your healing for anyone else's comfort. You do not have to apologize for needing time, for needing space, for needing to breathe again.

You only have to promise yourself one sacred thing: *"I will not abandon myself again."* The crossroads will wait for you. Your soul already knows the way. And when you are ready, you will rise.

Closing Whispers

(For the woman who stands trembling at the edge of everything she knew)

You do not have to choose today. You do not have to prove your pain. You do not owe the world your clarity, your plan, or your polished strength. Standing at the crossroads is a victory in itself. Still breathing? That's resilience. Still questioning? That's awareness. Still aching but refusing to go numb? That's power.

You are not weak for not knowing yet. You are not lost just because you don't have a destination. You are simply sacred, in the in-between. You are the woman who woke up in ruins and said, *"I'm still here."* You are the woman who stopped trying to carry what was never hers to hold. You are the woman who looked at the life she built and asked herself the bravest question of all: *"What if I deserve more than this?"*

There is no shame in staying if staying is done with truth. There is no shame in leaving if leaving is done with love. The only shame is in abandoning yourself to keep someone else comfortable.

So, take your time. Let the silence be your teacher. Let the ache reveal what's still sacred. And when it's time to choose, you'll know. Not because it will feel easy, but because it will feel honest.

You are not alone. You are not crazy. You are not too much. You are the storm and the stillness. You are the ache and the answer. You are the one who gets to decide what happens next, and that, my love, is where your power begins.

Soul Reflections

Questions to Sink Into

What does my deepest, most honest self believe about my marriage right now?

_____
_____
_____
_____
_____
_____
_____

What am I afraid will happen if I stay?

_____
_____
_____
_____
_____
_____

What am I afraid will happen if I leave?

_____
_____
_____
_____
_____
_____

What would I advise my daughter, my sister, my best friend if she were living my story?

_____

_____

_____

_____

_____

_____

_____

Which choice would be an act of love toward myself, not punishment?

_____

_____

_____

_____

_____

_____

_____

Sacred Mantra

"I trust myself to make hard choices. I honor my survival above anyone else's expectations. I will not abandon myself again."

Healing Ritual: The Crossroads Candle Ceremony

You Will Need:

- Two candles (one white, one red)

- Your journal

- Quiet sacred space

Instructions:

1. Place the two candles side by side.

2. Light the white candle for staying and rebuilding.

3. Light the red candle for leaving and starting anew.

4. Sit between them.

5. Close your eyes. Imagine walking each path in vivid detail.

6. Journal the emotions and visions that arise.

7. Whispers this prayer: *"I trust my soul to guide me where I am meant to go."*

8. Blow out both candles with reverence.

Chapter 03:

The Death of Illusions: Letting the Dream Go

The Funeral No One Attends

There are losses so deep that no language can fully touch them. When betrayal rips through a marriage, it is not only the heart that bleeds; it is the soul that fractures. The woman you were, the woman who believed, who trusted, who loved with her whole being…she doesn't just hurt.

She dies.

And the world around her does not notice the funeral. There are no flowers sent for the death of a dream. There are no casseroles brought over when you realize the man you loved with your entire being never loved you the way you loved him.

You are left to grieve in silence—a ghost mourning herself. And still expected to wake up the next day, fix your hair, go to work, smile at strangers, and pretend that the ground isn't crumbling beneath your every step.

No one prepares you for the way heartbreak makes everything heavier. Your skin becomes unbearable. Each step feels like you're dragging invisible chains, each breath shallow, barely enough to sustain the weight of loss pressing relentlessly on your chest. You become hyper-aware of your loneliness in crowded rooms, a lingering shadow in places that once felt safe and filled with love. The simplest tasks, from cooking dinner to choosing clothes, become battles waged against overwhelming exhaustion.

Rooms once filled with laughter feel hollow and sharp. The echoes of shared joy taunt you now, reminding you of everything you've lost. The bed you once shared feels like a cavern of absence, too vast and too silent to bear alone. You stare at the ceiling at 2:37 AM, heart pounding, trying to piece together the how, the why, the when.

Grieving the Man Who Never Was

Was it your fault? Were you not beautiful enough? Did you not love him the right way? Were you too much or not enough? You torture yourself with questions that have no answers, endlessly cycling through memories, searching for signs you missed or clues you ignored. Because deep down, you already know the only truth that matters: He chose to betray you. It had nothing to do with your worth. It was about his own brokenness, not yours. But knowing that doesn't make it hurt less. Knowing that doesn't unbreak the vows that now lie splintered at your feet. You are grieving the wedding day you thought meant something sacred, the gown that symbolized a future now shattered into irreparable fragments. You are grieving the whispered promises under starry skies, vows uttered with breathless sincerity now revealed as hollow words.

You are grieving the way you used to look at him, the way you used to believe that your love could protect you both from the monsters. You grieve the intimacy you shared, now a painful memory that feels more like betrayal than affection.

The deepest heartbreak is grieving a version of someone who never truly existed. You loved the idea of him. You loved the hope of him. You loved the potential he showed you before the masks fell away. And there is no shame in that. There is only sacredness. Because it means you were pure. You were real. You loved with a depth that many people spend their whole lives avoiding. Your love was not wasted, even if it was not reciprocated in the way you deserved.

But now, my love, you are being called into a different kind of love: A love that does not beg to be chosen. A love that rises first from within yourself. A love that says: *'I am enough, even alone. Especially alone.'* This love demands you confront your deepest fears and insecurities, embracing the raw truth of your own worthiness.

Resurrecting the Woman You Were Meant to Be

The death of an illusion is not tidy. It is messy. It will drag you through hell. It will leave you clawing at the walls of your own mind, desperate for an answer that softens the agony. It will test your resilience and question your sanity. You will find yourself screaming into pillows, pounding your fists against walls, weeping until there are no tears left.

But let me promise you this: You will survive this death. You will rebuild yourself from the ruins. Brick by brick, day by painful day, you will find strength you never knew existed. You will create a new dream, one that does not depend on another person for its breath, but thrives because it emerges from your deepest, most authentic self.

There will come a day when you do not wake up with a heart as heavy as stone. There will come a day when your reflection in the mirror looks back at you, not with shame, but with fierce pride. You will see the strength etched into your features, the warrior spirit in your eyes, the gentle resilience of a woman who faced the abyss and found a path forward. I died for a love that was never real. And I lived to create a love that is.

Today, you grieve. Allow yourself this sacred mourning. Tomorrow, you will rise. Not because you are ready. Not because the pain is gone. But because your soul was always built for resurrection. Your story does not end in betrayal. Your story is just beginning, illuminated by the courage it takes to walk away from illusions and step fiercely into the truth of who you are meant to become.

Closing Whispers

(For the woman who is mourning the dream, not the man)

This grief? It isn't pathetic. It isn't weakness. It's sacred. You're not just crying over a man. You're mourning a dream. A future. A version of love that lived only in your hope-filled heart.

You're allowed to ache for what never truly was. You're allowed to feel foolish, angry, shattered, hollow. And still... you're not broken. You are shedding illusions. You are burning down the lie that said love meant abandoning yourself to be "chosen." You are unlearning the belief that loyalty should ever cost you your peace.

It's okay that you miss the fantasy. It's okay that you loved who you thought he was. But it's even more okay to admit he wasn't that man. He never was. And your love deserved a safer home.

So tonight, if you need to scream into the dark, do it. If you need to collapse on the floor, do it. If you need to curl up with that wedding photo and sob until your soul shakes, do it. Let the pain speak. Let the illusion die.

And when the tears finally run dry, even for a moment, place your hand on your heart and whisper: *"I loved with everything I had. And that was never a mistake."* This is your funeral of false promises. This is your liberation from the lie. And when you rise, not perfectly, not completely, but truthfully... you'll rise with a power no illusion could ever hold.

Because now... now you see clearly. And that clarity is the beginning of your freedom.

Soul Reflection

Questions to Sink Into

What dream am I clinging to most tightly, and why does it terrify me to release it?

_____

_____

_____

_____

_____

_____

_____

How did the illusion protect me? What did it allow me to believe?

_____

_____

_____

_____

_____

_____

_____

In what small, tender ways can I begin to honor the truth of what happened, without shaming myself for wanting to believe in love?

_____

_____

_____

_____

_____

_____
_____

If I could whisper something to the woman I was before betrayal, what would I say to her?

_____
_____
_____
_____
_____
_____
_____

Sacred Mantra

"I honor my grief. I honor the woman who dreamed. I honor the woman who is rebuilding. I am still sacred, even in sorrow."

Healing Ritual: The Funeral of the Dream

Supplies:

- Journal or paper
- Candle
- Fireproof container
- Flower petals (optional)
- Small river stone (symbolizes permanence)

Instructions:

1. Write a raw, honest letter to the dream you are releasing. Spare nothing.

2. Hold the letter to your heart. Say: *"I bless the love I gave. I bless the love that will return to me a thousandfold."*

3. Light the candle.

4. Burn the letter in a fireproof container.

5. As it burns, sprinkle flower petals into the flames if you have them.

6. Keep the small river stone as a reminder: I survived the death of a dream, and I am still standing.

Chapter 04:

The Anatomy of Trust: Can It Be Rebuilt?

When the Foundation Cracks Beneath You

Trust is the bloodline of love. It is the sacred thread that weaves two souls together, unseen but unbreakable… until it is. When betrayal enters, it is not just the heart that breaks. It is the foundation itself that collapses. And you are left standing in the ruins, holding pieces so sharp they cut your palms, asking yourself the hardest question you will ever face: *"Can trust ever live here again?"*

Everyone talks about forgiveness. Everyone talks about fresh starts. But few talk about the brutal truth: When trust is shattered, it is not easily repaired. And sometimes… it shouldn't be.

Because real trust, true, soul-deep trust, is not rebuilt by words. Promises do not stitch it together. It is rebuilt action by action, breath by breath, day by brutal, aching day. And it must be rebuilt by both people, not just the one who was betrayed. Trust dies quickly. But its rebirth, if it happens at all, is slow. Painfully slow.

You will doubt him. You will doubt yourself. You will see betrayal hiding in innocent moments because your body remembers the violation even when your mind tries to move on. Every unexpected phone call, every late arrival, every unfamiliar scent, will send alarms through your nervous system, rekindling a terror that you desperately wish would vanish. Trust, once lost, leaves a scar deeper than anyone ever admits. Your heartbeat becomes an unreliable narrator, skipping beats every time the past whispers reminders of the devastation you endured.

The War Between Hope and Reality

You will wonder if you are foolish to stay. You will wonder if you are weak for wanting to believe in love again. You will punish yourself for staying, for leaving, for hoping, for hurting. Each choice will feel like stepping into thin air, hoping desperately that somehow your feet will find solid ground. Friends and family, with well-meaning words, will tell you how to feel, how to heal, how to move forward, but no one else has to live inside the haunted halls of your broken trust.

No choice will feel clean. No path will feel without pain. Because when betrayal happens, there is no simple *"fix."* There is only a long, grueling rebuilding or the courageous decision to walk away and rebuild yourself instead.

Here is the deepest truth: You are under no obligation to stay where your soul cannot breathe. If he is truly committed to change, you will not have to chase it. You will not have to beg for it. You will not have to monitor his every move like a prison warden guarding your own heart. Genuine remorse, true accountability, cannot be faked for long. It shows up in quiet, humble ways, in the consistent, unwavering truthfulness that feels unmistakably real. You will see it, feel it, and know it without second-guessing yourself. It will be a transparency that he offers willingly, fully aware of the fragility he has created.

He will do the work without needing to be asked. He will show you through relentless, humble, unglamorous consistency. He will be transparent not because you demand it, but because he knows he forfeited the right to your blind trust. And even then, you are still allowed to say: *"This is not enough for me."* You are allowed to set boundaries so fierce they startle you. You are allowed to require evidence not of perfection but of profound sincerity and transformation. And you are allowed, at any point, to step back and choose yourself instead.

Rebuilding Sacred Trust—Starting with You

Trust is sacred. It is holy ground. It is not a prize he earns back by saying the right things. It is a temple he must rebuild brick by brick, and it will take time, sweat, and sacrifice. Each brick placed with intention, each mortar carefully applied, is an act of repentance. It is his responsibility to acknowledge every fracture, every crack, every wound he inflicted and painstakingly, humbly, mend what he shattered.

And you? You owe yourself honesty. You owe yourself the freedom to say:

- *"I see the effort, but the wound is too deep."*

- *"I am choosing me."*

- *"I deserve peace more than I deserve proof that I am lovable."*

Because you are lovable, even if he never becomes the man you need. Because you are sacred, even if he cannot meet you where you stand. Because you are worthy, even if this story does not have the ending you once prayed for.

Sometimes trust can be rebuilt. Sometimes it cannot. Both are holy. Both are healing. Both are brave. The question is not: *"Can he make me trust him again?"* The question is: *"Can I trust myself again to know when it is time to stay, and when it is time to walk away?"*

You have survived the breaking. You will survive whatever comes next. But survival is not your only birthright. Joy, peace, laughter, ease, these belong to you, too. They are waiting patiently on the other side of trust, rebuilt or not. They are yours, fully and completely, regardless of the outcome.

Trusting again does not mean forgetting. It means moving forward fully awake to what you've endured, honoring your scars as marks of resilience rather than shame. It means listening to your intuition, your soul-whisper, even when the world around you questions your judgment. Trusting again means believing fiercely in your capacity to discern what is true, what is healing, and what is sacred.

You are more powerful than you know. You are more sacred than you remember. You will not lose yourself again. Not this time. And perhaps, if you dare, trust will live again, first within yourself, fiercely, powerfully, unshakably. From there, all else will flow.

Closing Whispers

(For the woman standing on the edge of maybe)

Trust is not a light switch. You don't just flip it back on because he says the right words. You don't owe your forgiveness to anyone who hasn't earned your safety. And most of all, you don't owe your soul to someone who cracked it open with their carelessness.

You are allowed to pause. To not know. To be unsure, even on the days you thought you'd made up your mind. You are not difficult. You are discerning. You are not bitter. You are protecting what is sacred.

Let them call you guarded. Let them say you're overthinking. Let them not understand because they were never the ones who lay awake at 3 a.m., chest tight, scanning for signs of betrayal in every silence.

You know what it costs to trust again. And this time, you'll spend that currency only on what is true. So, if you rebuild, let it be slow.

Let it be honest. Let it be yours.

And if you walk away, let it be bold. Let it be peaceful. Let it be your homecoming. Whatever you choose, choose with your soul, not your fear. Because trust is not just about them anymore, it's about you and how deeply you can trust yourself not to stay where your spirit cannot breathe.

This time, your heart will not be handed over blindly. It will be offered, if ever again, with the fierce love of a woman who knows her worth down to her bones. And if no one ever proves themselves again? You still win. Because you finally proved yourself to you.

Soul Reflections

Questions to Sink Into

What would rebuilding trust actually look like for me? What would I need to see consistently to feel safe again?

_____
_____
_____
_____
_____
_____
_____

Am I holding on because I truly see healing or because I am afraid to let go?

_____
_____
_____
_____
_____
_____
_____

If I trusted my own heart fully, what would it be telling me right now?

_____
_____
_____
_____
_____
_____
_____

What boundaries must be non-negotiable moving forward, no matter what?

_____
_____
_____
_____
_____
_____
_____

Sacred Mantra

"I trust myself first.

I honor my intuition.

I will not betray myself to keep someone else."

Ritual: The Mirror of Truth

What You Will Need:

- A mirror and a quiet, sacred space

Instructions:

1. Sit in front of the mirror. Look into your own eyes, deeply.

2. Whispers these words: *"I honor the woman who trusted. I honor the woman who was betrayed. I honor the woman who will never again abandon herself for love."*

3. Sit in silence for five minutes, breathing in trust, breathing out fear.

4. Journal whatever emotions rise.

Chapter 05:
The War Between Hope and Reality: Knowing When to Let Go

The Invisible Battlefield

There is a battlefield no one sees, the quiet war waged inside a broken heart. On one side: **Hope**. The relentless, trembling voice that whispers: *"Maybe it can be different this time. Maybe he means it now. Maybe the worst is over."* On the other side: **Reality**. The cold, aching truth that says: *"You have already seen who he is. You have already bled for this love. How many more pieces of yourself must you lose?"*

And you, caught in the middle, feel like a soldier forced to choose which part of yourself to betray: your faith in love, or your belief in yourself. It is the cruelest kind of agony. Because love teaches us to hold on. But survival sometimes demands that we let go.

Hope is not wrong. Hope is holy. It is proof that you still believe in the sacredness of connection. That even after betrayal, your soul longs for restoration, not revenge. You are not foolish for hoping. You are brave.

But there comes a moment… a sacred, brutal moment when you must ask: *Is my hope healing me or is it killing me?* There is no shame in wanting to fight for your marriage. There is no shame in wanting to heal together. There is only shame in abandoning yourself in the name of **"love."**

If staying costs you your sanity, your health, your dignity, your wholeness, then it is no longer love. It is self-destruction wearing a disguise. You do not owe anyone the slow death of your spirit. You do not owe loyalty to someone who betrayed your sacred trust. You do not owe someone forever who treated you like an option. You owe yourself everything you've been begging him to give you: honesty, loyalty, love, peace, safety.

And if he cannot meet you there, not in promises, but in action. Then, my brave soul, it is not your failure to let go. It is your victory. Choosing yourself is never a failure. It is a revolution.

The Sacred Decision to Let Go

It will not be easy. The heart will rebel. It will scream that you're giving up too soon. It will ache for the comfort of what once was, even if what once was is the very thing that broke you.

But listen deeper. Listen beneath the noise of fear and longing. There is another voice inside you, softer but stronger. The voice that says: You deserve love that doesn't leave bruises. You deserve trust; you don't have to earn it back every day. You deserve a home inside someone's heart where you don't have to fight to feel safe.

That voice is your soul. It will never lie to you. It whispers softly in moments of clarity, guiding you even through the thickest fog of doubt. Trust this voice, even if it's barely audible over your pain.

The war between hope and reality will not end in a clean victory. There will be grief either way. There will be nights you question your choice, nights when your pillow is soaked with tears and your heart feels impossibly heavy. There will be mornings when you wake with doubt, clinging to you like a shadow you can't shake.

But one day, after the storm has passed, after the ashes have settled, after you have cried every tear there was to cry, you will stand in the quiet dawn of your new life and realize: You didn't lose. You finally came home to yourself.

You will clearly see the strength it took to choose yourself over the ghost of what might have been. You will understand, perhaps for the first time, that letting go was not surrender; it was liberation.

The Victory Was You All Along

You will feel a peace deeper than anything you've known, a quiet knowing that you honored yourself, your heart, and your worth.

In this moment of clarity, you will realize that hope was never your enemy; it simply needed to be placed carefully within yourself. Hope now lives within your own heart, your dreams, your own healing journey. It no longer seeks fulfillment from empty promises or hollow words.

The victory was never about choosing between hope and reality. It was about realizing you deserve both: hope that is honest, kind, and a reality, and love that does not force you to compromise your soul. You have chosen wisely, bravely, and profoundly.

This war within you has ended, and in its wake, peace blooms, authentic, empowering, and undeniably yours. You will find yourself smiling again, laughing without reservation, dancing to music that moves your spirit. You will find beauty in solitude, strength in your newfound independence, and inspiration in the quiet, sacred spaces you create for yourself.

And perhaps most beautifully, you will find the courage to trust again, not blindly, but wisely. Trusting first in your own resilience, your own worth, and your unwavering ability to rebuild a life that honors the magnificence of who you have become.

Closing Whispers

(For the woman standing between what she prayed for and what she knows)

You were never weak for hoping. You were never foolish for believing. You were only ever human… wildly, beautifully, vulnerably human.

Hope was never your enemy. It kept you breathing when everything around you felt suffocating. It kept you standing when your knees wanted to collapse. It reminded you that your heart still beats and that in itself is sacred.

But now, it's time to ask yourself: *Is this hope helping you heal, or is it holding you hostage?*

You are not meant to stay in emotional purgatory, endlessly waiting for a version of him that only exists in your dreams. You are not meant to shrink for love, to bleed for comfort, to sacrifice your soul on the altar of **"what if."**

Letting go doesn't mean you didn't love him. It means you finally loved yourself more. You're not giving up, you're growing up. Spiritually. Emotionally. Energetically. You're choosing truth over fantasy. Peace over chaos. Self-worth over longing.

That is not a loss. That is a return. Back to you. Back to your own arms. Back to the woman who no longer begs to be chosen because she already knows she is.

So tonight, if your heart still aches, let it. Hold it gently. Whisper to it, *"I know this hurts, but we are not dying here."* Because tomorrow or the next day, or the one after that, you'll wake up and realize: *The war is over*. And you are the one who made it out alive.

Soul Reflections

Questions to Sink Into

What parts of me am I sacrificing to hold onto this relationship?

_____
_____
_____
_____
_____
_____
_____

What does my intuition tell me when I silence the fear and listen to my deepest truth?

_____
_____
_____
_____
_____
_____
_____

Am I trying to heal what cannot be healed because I am afraid of starting over?

_____
_____
_____
_____
_____
_____
_____

If I met myself as a stranger, would I tell her to stay or to run?

_____

_____

_____

_____

_____

_____

_____

Sacred Mantra

"My heart is sacred. My peace is sacred. I will not sacrifice myself to save what is already lost."

Healing Ritual: The Two Letters

What You Will Need:

- Two sheets of paper

- Pen

- A safe, quiet space

Instructions:

1. On one sheet, write a letter from your Hope:

    - All the reasons you want to stay.

    - All the dreams you still hold.

2. On the second sheet, write a letter from your Reality:

    - All the reasons you know this love may no longer be healthy for you.

- All the evidence your heart has been collecting.

3. Read both letters aloud.

4. Hold both letters to your heart. Say aloud: "I honor my hope. I honor my reality. I choose the path that leads me back to my own soul."

5. Keep both letters in a sacred place; they are witnesses to your courage.

Chapter 06:

When Grief Becomes the Healer: Loving the Woman Who Remains

Grief for the Love That Still Breathes

Grief is not just for death. Grief is for the dreams that died quietly in your hands. For the promises that were buried without a funeral. For the woman you were before the betrayal burned you alive. You are not only mourning the marriage. You are mourning the version of yourself who once believed she was enough. You are mourning the innocence that thought loyalty would beget loyalty, that love would be enough to protect you from devastation.

Grief, in this place, is not an event. It is a living, breathing creature you carry inside your chest every hour of every day. It wakes up with you. It eats with you. It crawls into bed beside you when he wraps his arms around you, and you wonder if those arms can ever feel like home again.

You are not crazy for grieving something that still breathes beside you. You are not weak for mourning what the world cannot see has died. You are a soul who trusted. You are a woman who loves with both hands open. And now you must love the woman who remains, even if she is unrecognizable at first.

Grieving the Old You

You may not realize it, but you are standing in a battlefield littered with the fragments of your old self: The woman who laughed freely without checking her partner's phone in the middle of the night. The woman who believed *"I love you"* was a sacred vow, not an empty echo. The woman who didn't second-guess every compliment, every touch, every text alert. The whole woman.

It is okay to cry for her. It is okay to miss her. It is okay to be angry at the world, at him, at yourself, at God. Your grief deserves space. It is not weak to say: *"I don't recognize myself anymore." "I miss the way I used to love without fear." "I miss believing I was enough."*

Grief is not your enemy. It is your witness. It is the proof that your love was real, that your heart was sacred, that your trust was not foolish; it was holy. You grieve because you loved with everything you had. You grieve because you were brave enough to trust.

Loving the Woman Who Remains

You may feel like a shattered mirror, a thousand pieces, sharp and unrecognizable. But hear this: Broken is not beyond repair. Shattered is not the end.

You are not here to become the woman you were before. You are here to become something more powerful: A woman who knows her own soul because she has walked through the fires of betrayal and lived to talk about it.

The woman who remains is bruised, yes. She is raw and bleeding. But she is also wiser. She is fierce in her honesty. She no longer begs to be loved; she knows that love must come freely, or it is not love at all.

Loving the woman who remains means: Speaking your truth even if your voice shakes, setting standards that honor your soul, even if it costs you the relationship. Looking at yourself in the mirror, puffy-eyed, broken-hearted, and saying: *"You are still worthy. You are still enough. You are still sacred."*

It means understanding that your healing is not contingent on whether he changes. Your healing is for you. Your happiness is not held hostage by his remorse, his apologies, his promises. You are not defined by the man who betrayed you. You are defined by the woman who chose to survive it.

The Sacred Rage

Let's tell the truth: You will feel rage. You will imagine burning everything to the ground. You will hate him. You will hate yourself for still loving him.

Let it rage. Your sacred rage is part of your healing. It is the fire that says, *"I deserved better." "I will never again tolerate less."* Your rage is not the enemy. It is the roaring voice of the woman inside you who refuses to stay small and broken.

Honor her. Scream into pillows. Write angry letters you never send. Run into the woods and sob until your knees hit the earth. You are allowed to grieve, and you are allowed to burn. And when the ashes settle, what remains will be the raw, undeniable truth of who you really are: A woman who loved deeply. A woman who lost herself in the fire. And a woman who will rise ... sacred, scarred, and sovereign.

You Are the Miracle You've Been Waiting For

No one is coming to save you. Not your husband. Not the version of him you hope still exists. Not time. Not another love. It is you. It has always been you. You are the miracle. You are the hero. You are the hope.

Loving the woman who remains means looking your grief in the eyes and saying: *"You will not destroy me. You will rebuild me."* It means kissing your own scars and saying: *"This is where the light got in."*

It means daring someday to trust again. Not because you forget what happened. But because you are stronger than what happened. You deserve love, yes. But first, you deserve your own.

And in loving yourself fiercely, unapologetically, you discover the profound truth: You were always enough. You were always worthy. The fire did not consume you; it forged you. It did not break you; it built you anew, resilient, fierce, and luminous with wisdom and grace.

Closing Whispers

(For the woman who aches, and dares to love herself anyway)

Grief is not a weakness. It is not a setback. It is not the end. Grief is your soul honoring what mattered. It's the echo of love, the cry of sacred loss, the whispered prayer of a heart that gave everything and still found itself here, breathing.

You are not wrong for missing who you used to be. You are not broken for mourning the version of you that believed love would protect her. You are becoming. And becoming is messy. It weeps. It rages. It aches in places too deep to name. But becoming also heals. It rises. It remembers.

The woman you see in the mirror now? She may look unfamiliar. But she is you... evolved, refined, ignited. She is not the same because she was never meant to be. You walked through fire and didn't burn out; you burned brighter. You held grief like a sacred offering and learned how to turn sorrow into strength. You looked at your own ruin and said: "Even here, I choose to love myself."

And that, my love, is what makes you unstoppable. So, when the grief visits again, and it will, welcome her like an old friend. Let her teach you. Let her soften you. Let her shape you into someone who doesn't just survive but thrives because the woman who remains is not less than the one who came before.

She is everything that was ever good and more. She is the miracle. She is the medicine. She is you, in all your sacred, luminous becoming.

Soul Reflections

Questions to Sink Into

What parts of myself do I miss the most before the betrayal?

_____
_____
_____
_____
_____
_____
_____

What would it feel like to grieve her, rather than shame myself for not "moving on"?

_____
_____
_____
_____
_____
_____
_____

How can I show sacred rage without destroying myself?

_____

_____

_____

_____

_____

_____

If I loved the woman I am right now, what would I say to her every morning?

_____

_____

_____

_____

_____

_____

Sacred Mantra

"Grief does not define me.

Betrayal does not break me.

I am the woman who survived the fire and learned how to heal herself."

Healing Ritual: Becoming Her Again

A sacred ceremony to honor your grief and call your soul home.

Purpose:

This ritual is for the quiet, trembling moment when you realize grief is not destroying you, it's rebuilding you. It helps you release the old version of yourself with love and reclaim the woman you're becoming with power.

You'll Need:

- A mirror (handheld or full-length, whatever feels personal)

- A white candle (symbol of healing and clarity)

- A bowl of warm water with salt (to cleanse and release)

- A pen and two small pieces of paper

- A soft towel or scarf

- Optional: soothing music, essential oils, or a comfort object like a blanket or crystal

Steps:

1. Create Your Space

Light the candle. Turn off distractions. Breathe deeply. Allow this to be a moment only for you. You are the sacred center of this ritual.

2. Acknowledge the Grief

On the first piece of paper, write down what you're grieving, the version of yourself you miss, the dreams that died, the things you wish you could have saved. Name it. Honor it.

Hold the paper to your heart and whisper: *"I see you. I remember you. I release you with love."*

Burn it safely in a fire-safe dish or tear it into small pieces and drop them into the salt water. Watch them dissolve or soak. Let it go.

3. Claim the Woman Who Remains

On the second piece of paper, write this: *"I am still here. I am still worthy. I am becoming her... whole, radiant, and mine."* Place this note in front of the mirror.

4. Mirror Invocation

Stand in front of the mirror. Look into your own eyes, not your face, not your pain. Your eyes. The window to the woman who remains.

Place your hand on your heart and speak aloud:

"I love the woman who remains. I honor her fire, her grief, her becoming. I do not need to return to who I was. I choose to rise as who I am now."

5. Saltwater Blessing

Dip your fingers in the warm, salted water and gently touch your forehead, heart, and hands, saying:

"With this, I cleanse the lies. I release shame. I call back my power."

6. Wrap & Receive

Wrap yourself in your scarf or towel. Sit in silence. Let the warmth hold you. Let your breath be your lullaby. Whisper softly: *"I am the woman I've been waiting for."*

7. Close the Circle

Blow out the candle with intention. Imagine the flame's light entering your heart, a spark that will never go out again.

Chapter 07:

The Art of Rebuilding:

Learning to Trust Yourself Again

There is a moment after the deepest betrayals when the world goes silent. The screaming, the sobbing, the endless replay of his lies, all dim. And what remains is terrifying: The silence inside yourself. The not knowing. The emptiness where certainty once lived. The desperate, trembling hands that used to know how to reach for hope but now hesitate.

You are no longer grieving him. You are grieving yourself. Who am I now? How do I trust again? How do I trust myself again? When he broke his promises, he didn't just break your heart. He shattered your belief in your own intuition. Because here's the truth no one talks about: When someone you love betrays you, the most brutal wound is not in them, it's in you.

"Why didn't I see it coming?" "How could I have been so blind?" "Was I not enough? Did I miss the signs?" "Was my love just ...stupid?"

You question everything. Every choice. Every instinct. Every feeling. You learn to mistrust not just the person who hurt you, but yourself. And that is the deepest kind of loneliness.

The Shattered Compass

Imagine your heart like a compass. Once, it pointed you to love, to dreams, to trust, to home. But betrayal smashes it. The needle spins wildly. You no longer know what is true or what is wishful

45

thinking. You no longer see if you're moving toward healing or another disaster. This is the loneliness no one sees. This is the silent panic no one talks about.

You smile. You say, *"I'm okay."* But inside, you're screaming: *"I don't know how to trust anything anymore…not even myself."*

The First Steps to Rebuilding

The healing doesn't begin when he apologizes. It doesn't begin when he changes (if he ever does). It doesn't begin when the memories finally stop ambushing you in the middle of the night. The healing begins the first time you decide to trust your own heart again, even if it's broken. Especially because it's broken, and it doesn't happen all at once. It happens in microscopic moments.

It happens when you listen to the smallest Whispers inside you, the ones that say:

"Get up, beautiful. One more day."

"Speak the truth, even if your voice shakes."

"You are allowed to feel all of this and still deserve love."

"You are still sacred, even in pieces."

Trusting Yourself Again: What No One Tells You

It will feel terrifying. You will second-guess every decision. You will fear being *"too much"* or *"too little"* all at once. You will ask for reassurance over and over and hate yourself for needing it. You will wonder if you are crazy. You are not crazy. You are wounded. And wounded hearts need tenderness, not shame. You are learning to walk with a broken leg. Of course, it feels unstable at first. You are learning to love yourself through the betrayal, not after it.

You are learning to breathe again with lungs that were filled with smoke. This is messy. This is hard. This is sacred. And you, even now, are worthy of your own love.

The Two Voices Inside You

There are two voices living inside you right now.

One is fear. Fear says: *"Never trust again. Wall up. Guard yourself. Assume the worst."* Fear says: *"Stay small. Stay bitter. Stay broken. It's safer here."*

The other is hope. Hope whispers, *"Maybe there is life after this."* Hope whispers, *"Maybe you can learn to love yourself even better than before."* Hope whispers, *"Maybe you will become even more beautiful because of the cracks."*

You do not have to banish fear. You do not have to shame yourself for feeling it. You simply have to choose, over and over again, to listen more closely to hope, even if hope is only a whisper at first. Even if hope feels foolish. Hope is not foolish. Hope is the strongest thing you will ever carry.

The Fear of Loving Again (Even Him)

Maybe you chose to stay. Maybe you are trying to rebuild a marriage that feels like a house burned to the ground. You will fear it happening again. You will fear trusting him. You will fear trusting yourself. And some days, your fear will be bigger than your love. That is okay. That is real.

Healing is not linear. Healing looks like holding fear in one hand and courage in the other and walking anyway. It looks like saying: "I am terrified. I am angry. I am still bleeding. But I choose to hope that there is still beauty left for me."

You Are Not Broken Beyond Repair

You are not crazy for still loving him. You are not stupid for wanting to believe in second chances. You are not foolish for daring to heal something that others say is too broken.

Your story is yours. And no matter what happens, whether you stay or go, your healing is already a miracle. Because you are fighting not just for a marriage. You are fighting for yourself.

You are fighting to believe that even in the ashes, even with the scars, even after the betrayal, you are still worthy of trust. You are still worthy of love. You are still worthy of yourself.

Every step you take towards rebuilding trust in yourself is an act of rebellion against the darkness that tried to claim you. Each tentative choice, each brave moment of vulnerability, each whispered affirmation is your soul reclaiming its rightful place within your heart. Remember, you were never truly lost; you were simply finding a new way home. And this time, the path leads directly back to you.

Closing Whispers

(For the woman learning to trust the sound of her own soul again)

There is no timeline for rebuilding. No checklist. No applause. No finish line. There is only this: You… standing, trembling, healing. Not because you were certain. But because you chose to believe in your voice again, even when it was a whisper.

Let them call you cautious. Let them call you slow. Let them call you guarded. What they don't see is that your heart was once shattered by someone you trusted most, and still, you chose to pick up the pieces.

You are not broken beyond repair. You are becoming a masterpiece that refuses to be rushed—a mosaic of truth, trauma, and quiet triumph. Rebuilding doesn't mean you always know what's right. It means you trust yourself enough to try again. To ask questions. To pause. To walk away if needed. To choose YOU without explanation, without apology.

Every time you choose your peace over your panic, every time you trust your body over someone else's excuses, every time you say, *"This doesn't feel right,"* you are coming home to the most loyal love you'll ever know: your own.

This is the art of trusting yourself again. It isn't loud. It isn't perfect.

But it is holy. And it is enough.

Soul Reflections

Questions to Sink Into

What does trusting myself mean to me now, after betrayal?

_____
_____
_____
_____
_____
_____
_____

What fears do I need to speak out loud so they lose their power?

_____
_____
_____

_____

_____

_____

_____

What small, brave thing can I do today to honor myself?

_____

_____

_____

_____

_____

_____

What would loving myself fiercely look like in this season?

_____

_____

_____

_____

_____

_____

Sacred Mantra

"My heart may be wounded, but it is still wise. I trust the woman I am becoming. I trust my healing. I trust my hope."

Healing Ritual: The Mirror of Self-Trust

This is a sacred practice to gently reconnect with your inner voice, the one that always knew the truth, even when you didn't want to hear it. This ritual isn't about dramatic breakthroughs; it's about the quiet, everyday rebuilding of self-trust, one breath, one choice, one whisper at a time.

To begin, gather a few things: a mirror (either handheld or full-length), a small white or gold candle for clarity and strength, a journal or piece of paper, a pen, and, if you like, a calming scent like lavender or eucalyptus, or soft instrumental music to create ambiance.

Start by lighting the candle and letting your breath slow. You're not here to perform, you're here to be present. As the flame flickers, feel yourself arriving in this moment. Stand or sit before the mirror, looking directly into your own eyes. Not your face, your eyes. The gateway. Let your breath deepen and, in your mind or out loud, call yourself back from all the places you've been scattered. Say: *"I am here. I am listening. I trust you, even if I'm still learning how."*

Next, open your journal and write down three lies you've told yourself since the betrayal. Lies like, *"I can't trust myself,"* or *"I was stupid,"* or *"I'll never know love again."* Then, and this part is important, cross them out boldly. Strike them through with intention.

Now, write three truths to take their place. Maybe something like, *"I am learning to trust myself every day."* Or, *"My love was honest, even if his wasn't."* Or, *"I am worthy of love, starting with my own."*

Return to the mirror once more and speak to the woman becoming. Say out loud: *"I am not who I was. I am who I am becoming."* Then, *"I honor my fear. But I follow my truth."* And finally, *"I trust myself ... gently, fiercely, again and again."*

When you feel ready, blow out the candle slowly. As the smoke curls into the air, imagine it carrying your old doubts with it. Let the new trust settle in your chest like a quiet warmth, a steady ember.

You are not starting from scratch. You are rising from sacred pieces, like a mosaic heart, made more beautiful by what it has survived. Trust her. She's coming home.

Chapter 08:

When Forgiveness Feels Impossible

There's a moment after betrayal when the word forgiveness feels like a slap to the face. When well-meaning advice stings deeper than the betrayal itself: *"You have to forgive to move on." "Forgiveness is for you, not for them." "Let it go already."*

As if forgiveness were some switch you could flip. As if healing your pulverized heart were a checklist you could simply tick off. They don't see you waking up at 3 AM, feeling the heaviness sitting on your chest, reliving conversations you thought were real but now feel like elaborate betrayals.

They don't see you crumbling when a song plays, when a text notification dings, when a flash of memory hits you like a blade to the ribs. They don't see how you bleed. And they sure as hell don't understand how impossible forgiveness feels when you are still gathering the broken bones of who you were.

The Myth of Quick Forgiveness

Forgiveness is often sold to us like a cheap fairytale: Forgive and forget. Move on. Smile wider. Pretend it didn't hurt that much. But real forgiveness, if you choose to offer it, isn't born from guilt or pressure. It's born from the ashes of your own rage. It's born after you've screamed and sobbed and written angry letters you never sent. It's born after you admit, even to yourself, how deeply you were hurt.

Forgiveness, true forgiveness, isn't weakness. It's the quiet rebellion of a soul refusing to carry what was never hers to hold.

You Don't Owe Anyone Your Healing Timeline

If you are too angry to forgive today, you are still in the process of healing. If today you can only manage to breathe without shattering, you are still healing. Forgiveness is not a performance. Forgiveness is not the erasure of your anger. Forgiveness is not letting them off the hook.

Forgiveness is about setting yourself free when you're ready, if you're ready. Not a moment before. Forgiveness is: A decision to reclaim your peace. An act of choosing yourself over bitterness. A way to say, *"You do not get to own my pain forever."*

Forgiveness is NOT: Saying what they did was okay. Pretending it didn't happen. Inviting them back into the same sacred spaces without boundaries. Sacrificing your sanity to keep the peace.

You can forgive and still walk away. You can forgive and stay, but with stronger walls around your soul. You can forgive and still cry. You can forgive and still have scars that ache when it rains.

Some days, you will want to forgive him, and then rage will flood you all over again. Some nights you will hold his hand, feel a flicker of love, and then remember the late-night whispers he shared with women who weren't you.

It will tear you in half. And it's okay to feel both. Healing doesn't mean you stop hurting. It means you learn to hurt without abandoning yourself.

If You Choose to Stay or Leave

If you choose to stay, understand that forgiveness will be a daily decision, not a one-time event. It will be a thousand small moments: When you catch yourself slipping into suspicion and breathe instead of accusing, when you feel the urge to weaponize the past and choose to speak from your wound, not your rage.

When you allow yourself to grieve the marriage you thought you had, even while building something new.

Forgiveness doesn't erase the past. It builds a bridge across it. A bridge you can walk over when you're strong enough, at your own pace, with your own bloody but beautiful feet.

If you choose to leave, forgiveness becomes your parting gift to yourself. Not because they deserve it. Because you deserve peace, you deserve mornings without waking to a sick feeling in your stomach. You deserve nights when your last thought isn't wondering who he's talking to. You deserve a life that doesn't revolve around managing someone else's broken promises.

Forgiveness in this case is not the same as reconciliation. It's liberation.

Your Forgiveness is Sacred

Whether you stay or go, whether you forgive or need more time, your journey is yours. There is no wrong way to heal. There is no shame in still bleeding. There is no shame in taking your time.

There is only this sacred truth: You are not your betrayal. You are not your bitterness. You are not your brokenness. You are your becoming. And whether or not you forgive them, forgive yourself. Forgive yourself for loving so hard. Forgive yourself for trusting so deeply. Forgive yourself for not seeing what you couldn't have known. Forgive yourself for the ways you hurt yourself while trying to survive.

You were doing the best you could with the broken compass you were handed. And that makes you not weak, but gloriously, ferociously, heartbreakingly brave.

You will feel rage, sorrow, longing, confusion, and numbness, sometimes all in a single hour. Let every emotion wash over you without judgment. Each feeling is part of the intricate tapestry of your healing. You are allowed to mourn what was lost. You are allowed to grieve openly for the woman you once were.

The journey toward forgiveness is deeply personal, fiercely intimate, and wholly yours. Your pain, your timeline, your healing… it belongs entirely to you. And no one else has the right to define what forgiveness should look like for you. Your heart knows its way home; trust it, even in the midst of a storm.

Closing Whispers

(For the woman who cannot yet forgive, and that is holy too)

You are not behind. You are not bitter. You are not doing it wrong. You are healing in the only way a soul can after it has been cracked open… slowly, messily, truthfully.

Forgiveness is not a race to be won. It is not a badge of moral superiority. It is not a spiritual bypass that says, *"None of this mattered."* It mattered. It hurt. It changed you. And that deserves reverence, not rushed redemption. Let the world preach easy forgiveness. Let them hand you clichés like bandages too small for the wound.

You? You are doing something more sacred. You are sitting with the weight of it. You are grieving, raging, feeling all of it without abandoning yourself. And that is holy. One day, you may choose to forgive. One day, you may not. But either way, your peace is not held hostage by anyone else's expectations.

You don't have to forgive on someone else's timeline. You don't have to forgive at all to be free. You only have to keep choosing yourself. So, if you can't offer forgiveness today, offer this: Grace. To your heart. To your healing. To the girl inside you who thought love would be enough. She didn't fail. She believed. And that is never something to be ashamed of.

Soul Reflections

Questions to Sink Into

What does forgiveness mean to me personally, not what others have told me it should mean?

_____
_____
_____
_____
_____
_____
_____

Am I pressuring myself to heal faster than my soul can manage?

_____
_____
_____
_____
_____
_____
_____

What would reclaiming my peace on my terms look like?

_____
_____
_____
_____
_____
_____
_____

What am I ready to forgive myself for today?

_____

_____

_____

_____

_____

_____

_____

Sacred Mantra

"I forgive myself for believing I had to be perfect to be loved. I forgive myself for the ways I bled for love. I am worthy of peace, no matter what anyone else has done."

Healing Ritual: The Burn Letter of Release

This sacred fire ritual is designed to help you release resentment, honor your grief, and reclaim your energy, even if forgiveness still feels far away. Begin by gathering a few intentional items: a piece of paper and a pen, a safe candle or fire-safe bowl, a lighter or matches, and a bowl of water or a patch of earth where you can bury the ashes. You may also wish to set the mood with music, incense, or calming oils ... anything that makes this moment feel sacred.

Find a quiet space where you won't be interrupted. Light your candle and close your eyes. Breathe deeply, allowing whatever needs to rise to the surface without judgment. This is a space for truth, not performance. When you're ready, take the paper and begin your letter with the words, *"This is everything I never said out loud..."* Let it all pour out ... the betrayal, the rage, the sorrow, the guilt, the shame, the ache of wanting something you didn't get. Write uncensored, unfiltered. Let your soul speak freely. And when you've said it all, end your letter with: *"I release this pain from my body. I release their hold on my peace. I choose me."*

If you feel ready, read the letter aloud. This isn't to reopen the wound but to bear witness to say to yourself: I was there. I felt this. I survived. Let your voice hold space for your own pain, without shame. Then, when you're ready, carefully light the letter on fire, or if fire is not safe, tear it into pieces with deliberate intention. Watch as the smoke rises or the paper dissolves, not as destruction, but as liberation. Say aloud as you release it: *"I am not this pain. I am not the one who betrayed. I am free."*

Once the burning is complete, drop the ashes into water or return them to the earth. Feel the energy shift. It may be subtle, like a lightness in your chest or a sigh that feels like truth. No, this ritual doesn't end your healing, but it does mark a powerful letting go.

To close, speak this truth into the space around you and within you: *"I don't have to forgive yet. I only have to keep choosing myself. That is enough."*

And it is.

Chapter 09:

Mourning the Marriage. You Thought You Had

There is a grief that no one prepares you for, a grief without a funeral, a grief without flowers or condolences. It is the death of a marriage that still breathes beside you. It's the crumbling of a life you built in your mind, the slow, excruciating realization that what you thought was real… the vows, the late-night whispers, the tender promises, were not the whole truth.

You are mourning something invisible. You are mourning a love story that you lived with your whole heart, only to find you were reading from different scripts all along.

How do you explain the death of a future? How do you put into words the ache of realizing you loved harder, deeper, more loyally than they did? How do you grieve a person who still shares your bed but not your soul? There is no neat, acceptable way to mourn a betrayal. You cry in the shower so no one can hear. You smile at the grocery store clerk with hollow eyes. You laugh at a joke but feel it rattle around in your emptiness. You scroll through old photos and feel the blade twist in your gut … the smiling faces, the hands intertwined…the illusion of safety that now feels like mockery.

You loved with a truth that deserved to be met equally. And it wasn't. And now you are left with a thousand unanswered questions screaming inside your chest.

The Quiet Violence of Betrayal

Infidelity isn't just a physical betrayal. It's an emotional war that leaves invisible scars: The nights you stayed up worrying while they texted someone else *"goodnight."* The birthdays you celebrated while they entertained strangers in their minds. The family vacations you planned while they planned conversations with others. The vulnerable parts of yourself you offered while they offered pieces of themselves elsewhere.

It's not just about sex. It's about safety. It's about trust. It's about home. And when that is shattered, you don't just lose a marriage. You lose the version of yourself who believed she was safe there.

She deserves to be mourned too... the woman who believed, the woman who trusted without question, the woman who thought she was enough. You are allowed to cry for her. You are allowed to be angry for her. You are allowed to miss her. You are allowed to rebuild her... stronger, wiser, softer where it matters, and fiercer where it doesn't.

You did not lose her completely. She is not gone. She is evolving. Every tear, every heartbreak, every sleepless night is the forging of a woman more powerful than betrayal could ever imagine.

You will feel contradictions clawing at your heart: Loving him but hating what he did. Missing the good times but despising the lies.

Wanting to heal but wanting him to feel your pain. Craving closeness but flinching at his touch.

This is the chaos of grief. This is the war of mourning, a half-dead marriage. You are allowed to hold all of it at once. You are allowed to not make sense. You are allowed to simply survive today.

And then, the Breakdown Over a Damn Sock

Because here's the thing they don't tell you in therapy: sometimes your grief will come for you in the middle of laundry day. It won't wait for the perfectly candlelit moment of reflection. No, it will sneak attack you when you find a single sock you folded for him, and suddenly you're sobbing on the floor like it's a damn Shakespearean tragedy.

Or you'll be pumping gas and remember the road trip you planned for your anniversary that he canceled last-minute *"for work,"* and you'll fantasize, just for a moment, about keying his car. (You won't. But you could. And that tiny thought feels deliciously criminal.)

Grief has a sense of humor. A dark, sarcastic one. And you're allowed to laugh through the rage. Cry while making pancakes. Feel completely fine at noon and like you're dying by 3:17 p.m.

That's not instability. That's being human.

A Different Kind of Love Story

Maybe, just maybe, this isn't the end of your story. Maybe it's the messy middle. Maybe it's the sacred burning down before the rebirth. Maybe you are being carved open so you can love yourself in ways no one else ever could.

Whether you stay or go, whether you rebuild with him or rebuild without him, your new love story begins inside yourself. It begins when you realize that your worth is not defined by anyone's inability to cherish it.

You are not broken because he broke his promises. You are not unlovable because he loved recklessly. You are not too much. You are not too little. You are a fierce, blazing, beautiful being whose soul was never meant to be swallowed by betrayal.

You are allowed to mourn. You are allowed to scream. You are allowed to ache. And then, when you're ready, you are allowed to rise.

Closing Whispers

(For the woman who buried her future with no eulogy)

There are no sympathy cards for this. No black dresses, no casseroles. Just you, mourning a marriage that still breathes beside you, and a dream that died in silence.

This kind of grief is invisible to the world… but not to your soul. Your soul saw the slow unraveling. It felt the shift in his eyes, the weight in your chest, the way your laughter began to shrink.

And still, you stayed. You fought. You believed. You were never foolish for loving with both hands open. You were holy. So, mourn her, the version of you who thought love meant safety. The woman who believed the vows. The woman who held her breath, hoping this time would be different.

Let the tears come. Let the ache stretch wide.

You are not broken because it broke. You are brave because you're still here. This grief is not weakness. It is evidence of how deeply you loved, and how fiercely you're learning to love yourself now. You do not have to explain it. You do not have to minimize it. You do not have to rush through it to make others comfortable.

This is your funeral. And from it, something sacred is being born. You. Still here. Still breathing. Still becoming.

Soul Reflections

Questions to Sink Into

What dreams or expectations am I grieving right now?

_____

_____

_____
_____
_____
_____
_____

What version of myself am I mourning?

_____
_____
_____
_____
_____
_____

What would honoring that loss look like with love, not shame?

_____
_____
_____
_____
_____
_____

How can I begin to write a new story for myself, even if I don't know the ending yet?

_____
_____
_____
_____
_____
_____

Sacred Mantra

"I honor the woman who loved without armor. I mourn the dreams that didn't survive. I trust that a new life, more aligned with my soul, is already taking root inside me."

Healing Ritual: The Funeral for the Marriage, You Thought You Had

This symbolic ritual is a sacred space to grieve not just what has ended, but what never truly existed —the illusion, the hope, the story you clung to. It is a ceremony for mourning and release, as well as for honoring the brave heart that dared to believe in forever.

To begin, gather a few items: a black or white candle to represent mourning and clarity, a small box, jar, or envelope to hold your grief, several slips of paper, a pen, and a flower or small token to symbolize your rebirth. Find a quiet place where you won't be interrupted. Light the candle and allow yourself to sit in stillness. Watch the flame and let it symbolize both the destruction and the beginning. Breathe deeply and let grief rise in its own time, no judgment, no rushing. This is sacred space.

Take the slips of paper and begin to write down every part of the marriage you believed you had, the future you envisioned, the promises that were made, the dreams that died. Let each entry begin with the words, *"I grieve…"* Say the unsaid. Name what was lost. *"I grieve the anniversary trips we'll never take." "I grieve the safety I thought I had." "I grieve the man I believed he was."* Let your truth spill, without censoring.

Then, take a moment to honor the version of you who believed. Write a final note to your past self, the woman who tried, who loved deeply, who didn't yet know the truth. Tell her she mattered. Thank her for her courage. Maybe you write, *"Thank you for loving so deeply. I will carry your heart with me, but I am ready to become someone new now."* Once finished, place all of your papers into the box, envelope, or jar. This is your symbolic burial, a funeral for the dream.

Hold the container to your heart and speak softly into the silence: *"I release what never truly was. I let go of the illusion so I can rise in truth. This grief is sacred. This ending is mine."* When you feel ready, place the box somewhere meaningful. You might bury it in the earth, tuck it away in a drawer, or burn it safely as a final act of release.

To complete the ritual, place your flower or symbolic token beside the candle. Let it represent your becoming, the woman rising from the ashes. Speak this truth aloud: *"I mourned what was never real. Now I make space for what is. I honor my grief. And I choose me."* Blow out the candle and watch the smoke drift upward, carrying with it all the pieces you no longer need to carry alone.

This is not just an ending. It is the beginning of your return to yourself.

Chapter 10:

The First Breath After the Storm

You don't notice it at first. It doesn't come with fireworks or declarations. There is no applause, no obvious sign that something inside you has shifted. It happens quietly. One morning, in the thick of your mourning, you catch yourself laughing at something small, and the sound startles you.

It happens when you feel the warmth of the sun on your skin and, for a fleeting second, you don't feel the heaviness crushing your ribs. It happens when you realize you went a whole hour without replaying the betrayal in your mind.

When you notice you are breathing, not just surviving, but breathing. The first breath after devastation is timid, fragile. It is filled with doubt and uncertainty. But it is also filled with life.

Tiny Resurrections

Healing doesn't come all at once. It sneaks up on you in fragments:

A day you don't check his phone. A night you sleep through without waking up in tears. A conversation where you say exactly what you mean without apologizing for it.

These are tiny resurrections. Proof that even when you feel buried under the wreckage, your soul keeps pushing toward the light. You are not broken beyond repair. You are breaking open into something wider, braver, and truer.

These small victories deserve to be celebrated, even if only quietly acknowledged. Each one is evidence of your resilience, of your relentless courage to reclaim yourself from the shadows of betrayal.

There is a strange guilt that comes with the return of joy, as if your grief demands constant devotion. As if laughing, smiling, living, somehow betrays the hurt you carry. But you are allowed to hold both. You are allowed to miss what you lost and embrace what is growing. You are allowed to honor your sadness and welcome your joy.

Healing isn't betrayal. It's survival. It's rebellion. It's your soul refusing to stay dead. Your joy is sacred; it honors the depth of your pain by proving that, despite everything, you are still capable of feeling happiness.

Also, let's be honest, joy isn't always some divine ray of light beaming from the heavens. Sometimes it's just finally getting your eyeliner even on both sides. Sometimes it's dancing like a maniac to Beyoncé in your kitchen while holding a spoon like a mic. Sometimes it's realizing you didn't think about him for three straight hours... and immediately thinking, holy shit, maybe I'm okay?

Healing will confuse you like that. You are becoming a woman who knows her own strength, even when her voice trembles. You are becoming a woman who understands that trust begins within herself first. You are becoming someone who doesn't just rebuild but who reinvents her entire foundation.

Maybe he stays. Maybe he proves himself worthy. Perhaps he doesn't. But the truth is: Your healing was never meant to depend on someone else's ability to change. Your healing is your own. Your life is your own. Your happiness is your birthright, not a reward for someone else's good behavior.

You are transforming into a woman who can look in the mirror and see beauty in the scars, strength in the vulnerability, and wisdom in the lessons painfully learned. You are becoming someone who can finally say, with conviction, "I am enough."

The Choice Ahead

At some point… not today, maybe not even tomorrow … you will face a quiet but fierce choice: To stay trapped in the ruins or to rise from them, even if you rise shaky and bruised and terrified.

This is not about pretending everything is okay. It's about deciding that even if it isn't okay right now, you will not let this chapter be the end of your story. This choice will not feel easy or neat. It will feel raw, painful, and uncertain. But it is also brave and necessary. You are choosing life, even if life right now is messy, complicated, and uncertain. You have survived the storm. Now, with shaking hands and a battered heart, you take your first breath after it. And that breath, no matter how small, is a revolution.

It is the beginning of your reclamation, your return to yourself. It is the whispered declaration that you will no longer live defined by someone else's actions. You will no longer let betrayal dictate your worth or your capacity to love.

In this breath, you are reclaiming your soul. You are reclaiming your power. You are reclaiming your joy, your laughter, your dreams, your future. And perhaps, most importantly, you are reclaiming your right to be deeply, profoundly, unapologetically alive again.

Closing Whispers

(For the woman whose breath was stolen and who dares to breathe again)

You don't need to roar to be rising. You don't need to smile to be healing. You don't need to dance just yet.

But breathe even if it's shallow, even if it's shaky. Even if it's interrupted by sobs, that breath is your beginning. The storm didn't break you. It revealed you.

You are not here to be anyone's aftermath. You are here to be your own becoming. Let the world underestimate the woman who's learning to breathe again.

She is dangerous. She is divine. She is home to her own damn self now.

Soul Reflections

Questions to Sink Into

When was the last time I felt even a flicker of joy, even if it was brief?

_____

_____

_____

_____

_____

_____

_____

What parts of me have begun to heal without me even realizing it?

_____

_____

_____

_____

_____

_____

_____

Where am I still holding onto guilt for feeling happy?

_____

_____

_____

_____

_____

_____

_____

What would it look like to allow myself tiny, guilt-free moments of peace today?

_____

_____

_____

_____

_____

_____

_____

Sacred Mantra

"I honor every broken piece of myself. I honor every new bloom of life. I breathe, I rise, I reclaim my soul."

Healing Ritual: The First Breath Ceremony

A quiet ritual to mark the moment you realize you are breathing again and reclaiming your life, breath by breath.

You'll Need:

- A white candle (for clarity and soul rebirth)

- A blank piece of paper and a pen

- A quiet space (early morning or dusk is ideal)

- A glass of water

- Your breath, nothing more sacred than that

Steps:

1. Light the Candle

Let the light symbolize your return, not to your old life but to your soul.

2. Place Your Hand Over Your Heart

Close your eyes. Feel your breath. Don't try to control it. Just notice it. The inhale. The exhale. The miracle of still being here.

Say aloud: *"I am still here. I am still breathing. I am still becoming."*

3. Write This One Line on Paper:

"My life begins again today." Below it, write what you're ready to breathe life back into joy, creativity, sex, laughter, trust, peace, your sense of self, whatever stirs in your chest.

4. Drink the Water

As a symbol of cleansing. Of flowing forward. Of nourishing the woman who dared to keep going.

5. Sit in Silence for Three Full Breaths

With each breath, repeat:

"I inhale peace. I exhale the past." "I inhale power. I exhale pain."

"I inhale me."

6. Blow Out the Candle

As you do, say: *"This chapter begins with breath. And I am ready for it."*

Chapter 11:

Rebuilding Trust:

Brick by Broken Brick

Trust.

A word so small you can whisper it, but so heavy it can crush an entire life when it falls apart.

When trust is shattered, it doesn't just tear apart the space between you and him, it detonates something inside you, too. It leaves you questioning your judgment, your worth, your sanity. It makes you wonder if love itself was ever real or just a cruel trick your heart played on you.

The worst betrayal wasn't his lies. It was what his lies did to your ability to believe in yourself.

Long before the texts you found, long before the gut feelings you silenced, there were tiny moments, moments when your body whispered, *"Something isn't right,"* and you told yourself, *"I'm overthinking." "I'm insecure." "If I just love him harder, this will pass."*

You betrayed yourself in the name of loyalty. You handed over your intuition like a sacrificial offering on the altar of *"keeping the peace."* You made yourself smaller, quieter, easier … so you wouldn't lose him.

But love, hear me: You were never too much. You were never wrong for sensing the storm coming. You were never foolish for loving fully. You were doing what you were taught, that a woman's love should be limitless, even if it costs her herself.

Now, the real work begins: Rebuilding not just your trust in him, but also rebuilding your sacred, broken trust in yourself.

Learning to Trust Yourself Again

It starts painfully, awkwardly, like learning to walk again after a terrible injury. You second-guess your instincts. You doubt your own wisdom. You wonder if you'll ever know how to feel safe again.

You will.

But first, you must become fierce about protecting your spirit. Rebuilding trust in yourself looks like: Listening when your body recoils from someone's touch, even if they're *"sorry."* Honoring when your heart whispers, *"This doesn't feel right,"* instead of drowning it out with hope. Setting boundaries so firm they could withstand hurricanes, not because you expect people to betray you, but because you refuse to betray yourself again.

Every time you say *"No more"* to something that harms you, you pour gold into the cracks of your broken soul. Every time you believe in yourself, you sew a torn piece of your spirit back together.

Can He Be Trusted Again?

This is the question that haunts you. Can a man who shattered your world ever rebuild it? Can a man who looked you in the eyes and lied hold your heart with reverence again?

Maybe. Maybe not.

The real question is: Does he even deserve the chance?

Not because you are bitter. Not because you are punishing him. But because you are learning to honor yourself the way you always deserved to be honored. True repentance doesn't hide behind flowers or hollow promises. It shows up in consistency, in transparency, in sitting beside your brokenness without running away or blaming you for bleeding.

True repentance is:

- Him feeling your pain like it's his own.

- Him dismantling his own ego.

- Him doing the soul work, not just to win you back, but to become a man worthy of being loved by a woman like you.

You owe it to yourself to watch with clear, open eyes, not through the veil of hope, but through the lens of hard-earned wisdom.

The War Between Hope and Reality

You will ache to believe him. You will cling to his moments of sweetness like lifeboats in the wreckage. You will convince yourself that maybe, maybe the nightmare is finally over.

But hope without evidence is a dangerous addiction. It feeds the fantasy while starving the reality. This doesn't mean you must stop hoping. It means you must tether your hope to proof, to actions, not words. You are not stupid for hoping. You are brave for hoping and demanding better.

Also, let's be real: You'll have moments where you start to trust again, then suddenly catch yourself Googling *"how to install hidden cameras in houseplants"* or thinking, If I had a second phone, would that be crazy or just emotionally resourceful?

This is the reality of healing… messy, raw, occasionally petty. And still? Beautiful.

If He Is Truly Changing

Real change in a man who betrayed you feels like:

- He tells the truth even when it's uncomfortable.

- He volunteers transparency without being asked.

- He seeks healing for himself without you dragging him to it.

- He holds you through the aftershocks of your pain without defensiveness, without rushing your healing.

If you have to remind him, beg him, monitor him, he hasn't changed. A man who truly repents doesn't need convincing. He is already on his knees, rebuilding the temple he desecrated.

Your Worth Was Never in His Hands

You were worthy the day you were born. You were worthy before he said your name in love, and you are worthy even after he spoke it in lies. You are worthy whether he chooses you every day or whether he walks away like a ghost into someone else's arms.

You are worthy even if you wake up alone. You are worthy even if you rise from this with nothing but your own bloodied but beating heart. Your worth has never been dependent on the way someone else loved you. It has always been your birthright.

If you stay, let it be because he is building with you, not because you are building alone and begging him to notice. If you stay, let it be because your heart feels safe again, not because you are clinging to the memory of a man who no longer exists. If you stay, let it be because the love being rebuilt honors your spirit, not because you are too afraid to start over.

You are allowed to stay. You are allowed to leave. You are allowed to choose yourself. No matter what.

Brick by brick, piece by painful piece, your trust is rebuilt... slowly, carefully, intentionally. Each brick is a promise kept, each stone a truth spoken, each beam a boundary respected. And in the quiet, hard-earned strength of your reconstruction, you find yourself again: wiser, braver, stronger than ever before.

Closing Whispers

(For the woman rebuilding from splinters)

You are not weak for trusting again. You are not naive for hoping. You are not foolish for wanting your heart to feel safe again.

You are brave. Brave enough to feel the cracks in your soul and still reach for healing. Brave enough to demand evidence over excuses. Brave enough to say, *"I love you,"* with one hand... and *"I will leave if I must,"* with the other.

You are not rebuilding a version of love that asks you to shrink. You are rebuilding a love that expands in truth, in honor, in sacred safety, starting with the way you love yourself. This trust? This is the new version of it. It belongs to you now. Guard it. Honor it. Let no one near it who hasn't earned it.

Soul Reflections

Questions to Sink Into

What early warning signs did I once ignore, and how can I honor them now?

_____

_____

_____
_____
_____
_____
_____

What does my body feel when I am safe versus when I am being lied to?

_____
_____
_____
_____
_____
_____

What would loving myself fiercely and unapologetically look like today?

_____
_____
_____
_____
_____
_____

What actions, not words, do I need to see before offering my trust again?

_____
_____
_____
_____

_____

_____

What would it feel like to trust myself again fully?

_____

_____

_____

_____

_____

_____

_____

Sacred Mantra

"I am rebuilding my soul brick by brick, even if my hands are shaking. I trust myself. I honor my own sacred knowing."

Healing Ritual: The Trust Brick Ceremony

A symbolic ritual to begin rebuilding trust in yourself, one truth at a time.

You'll Need:

- 5 small stones, wood pieces, or paper "bricks"

- A marker

- A safe space to sit quietly

- A candle (white or gold)

- A journal (optional)

Steps:

1. Light the Candle

Let this be the flame that lights your rebuilding, one truth at a time.

2.   Label Your Bricks

On each "brick," write one truth you now stand on, one truth you believe about yourself, your worth, your healing.

Examples:

- I can trust myself again.

- I am worthy of safe love.

- I am allowed to walk away.

- My voice is sacred.

- I no longer betray myself to keep the peace.

3.   Build Your Foundation

Stack or line up the bricks in front of the candle. With each one, say aloud: *"This truth belongs to me now."*

4.   Seal the Ritual

Place your hand on your heart and say: *"I am no longer rebuilding for him. I am rebuilding for me."*

5.   Keep the Bricks Visible

Place them on your nightstand, altar, or journal. Let them remind you what your new foundation is made of: truth, choice, and sacred power.

Chapter 12:

When Loving Them Feels Like Losing Yourself

There's a moment after betrayal that splits your soul into two: The part that still clings to the memories, to the dream, to the man you thought he was. And the part that is slipping away, drowning silently in a sea of sadness, shrinking smaller and smaller each time you swallow your hurt to keep the peace.

You start to wonder: *"How much of myself can I sacrifice before there's nothing left to give?"* *"How much can I bend before I finally break?"* This is the bleeding ground where heartbreak meets survival.

The Slow Death of Self-Sacrifice

At first, you think loving him harder will fix it. You convince yourself that if you're more patient, more forgiving, more understanding, more silent, more beautiful, more accommodating, he will choose you again.

But with every compromise, a piece of you quietly dies:

- The part that used to laugh freely without second-guessing.

- The part that used to dream wildly, selfishly, boldly.

- The part that once knew her worth without needing anyone to validate it.

You start shrinking yourself to fit inside the spaces he left empty. You become a ghost of the woman you once fought so hard to become. Each time you mute your laughter, hide your brilliance, or silence your desires, another part of you fades into the shadows, slowly becoming unrecognizable even to yourself.

And the truth is? It's not just painful, it's maddening. One day, you'll look in the mirror while brushing your teeth and think, Who the hell is she? And when did she stop listening to Beyoncé while flossing and start crying into her electric toothbrush instead?

Yeah. That's the moment grief gets weird and hilarious in the most messed-up way.

The Lies We Tell Ourselves to Survive

We lie to ourselves to make the unbearable feel bearable:

- *"He's trying his best."*

- *"It's my fault too."*

- *"If I just work harder, he'll see my worth again."*

Each lie is a paper cut. Alone, it stings. Together, they bleed you dry. We tell ourselves these lies because the truth that someone we loved could wound us so carelessly is a truth too heavy to hold some days.

But queen, you are stronger than you think. You can carry the truth. You can survive it. And on the other side of that survival, you can rebuild a life so radiant that even you won't recognize it yet.

How to Know When You Are Losing Yourself

Losing yourself doesn't happen all at once. It happens slowly, drip by drip, like water hollowing stone.

- You'll notice it in subtle, devastating ways:

- You second-guess your every word, worried how he'll react.

- You stop doing the things you love because you don't want to upset him.

- You silence your own needs to avoid more conflict.

- You start feeling invisible even when you're right beside him.

- You find yourself apologizing for being hurt, for crying, for simply feeling.

If you've lost yourself, it's not because you were weak. It's because you loved so fiercely that you were willing to sacrifice yourself on the altar of second chances.

But love that costs you yourself isn't love. It's slow annihilation.

Choosing Yourself Without Guilt

You are allowed to want a love that feels safe. You are allowed to want a partner who guards your heart as if it were his own, not because you are fragile, but because you are sacred.

You are allowed to say: *"I deserve more than this." "I deserve to love and be loved without fear."* You are allowed to leave the version of him that chose betrayal behind, even if he's standing in front of you now, begging you to stay. You do not owe your life to a man who didn't treasure your heart the first time. You owe your life to yourself.

And let's be honest, it's exhausting trying to carry a relationship on your back while also pretending not to notice the emotional landmines he left scattered across your home like passive-aggressive confetti.

You don't need to smile through that. You need to walk through it or away from it, with your damn crown on straight.

If You Stay, Stay Whole

If you choose to stay and rebuild, remain a whole woman, not a half-loved fragment of yourself. Stay without silencing your pain. Stay without pretending it didn't happen. Stay without lowering the standards your soul is screaming for.

Stay only if the man beside you is willing to meet you, wounded heart to wounded heart, soul to soul, without defense, without lies, without manipulation. Stay if he is building a new foundation with you, brick by honest brick.

Otherwise, gather your shattered heart, gather the tiny embers of your once blazing spirit, and rise even if you rise alone. Even if your voice trembles. Even if you are the only one who believes in your worth at first.

Choose you. Choose your wild, beautiful, battered heart. Choose your life.

Your Soul Was Never Meant to Shrink for Love

You were born to expand. To thrive. To take up glorious space in this world. You were never meant to be an afterthought, a shadow, a secret. You were never meant to beg for scraps of loyalty from someone who couldn't see the infinite galaxy in your soul.

There is a life waiting for you, one built on truth, on honor, on sacredness. Whether you rebuild it with him or rebuild it for yourself, know this: You are not lost. You are coming home. And the woman you are becoming?

She will be unstoppable. You will reclaim every corner of yourself that you willingly surrendered. You will rediscover the laughter you thought had disappeared forever. You will remember the dreams you tucked away in the name of love and bring them forth into the light again, stronger and brighter than ever before.

And someday, sooner than you imagine, you will look back and understand the depth of your resilience. You will see the profound strength it took to choose yourself, even when it meant stepping into the unknown. Loving yourself enough to walk away or loving yourself enough to rebuild... this, my beautiful heart, is the most courageous act of all.

Closing Whispers

(For the woman who forgot herself while trying to be enough for someone else)

You are not selfish for wanting more. You are not broken for feeling lost. You are not weak for loving someone who didn't know how to love you back. You simply believed in him, in love, in the dream. And that belief is not your shame. It is your glory. But now it's time to believe in someone else... you.

The woman who sacrificed her voice? She is coming back. The one who muted her sparkle? She is lighting fires again.

This time, you do not shrink. This time, you expand. This time, love will not cost you your soul because you will never abandon yourself again.

Soul Reflections

Questions to Sink Into

Where have I sacrificed pieces of myself in this relationship?

_____
_____
_____
_____
_____

_____
_____

What dreams, passions, and joys have I put on hold for the sake of love?

_____
_____
_____
_____
_____
_____

What would loving myself without fear look like?

_____
_____
_____
_____
_____
_____

Am I staying because love is being rebuilt or because I'm afraid of starting over?

_____
_____
_____
_____
_____
_____

Sacred Mantra

"I do not have to lose myself to love someone else. I am whole. I am sacred. I am home within myself."

Healing Ritual: The Return to Self-Ceremony

A sacred act of calling yourself back from the places you gave too much away

You'll Need:

- A mirror (handheld or full-length)

- A candle (red for fire, pink for self-love, or white for clarity)

- A pen and a paper

- A bowl of water

- Optional: soft music, incense, or a comforting item

Steps:

1. Create Sacred Space

Light your candle. Stand or sit in front of the mirror. Let this be your sacred witnessing.

2. Write the Surrender

On the paper, write this sentence at the top: *"These are the pieces of myself I gave away..."*

Then list them. Your laughter. Your voice. Your self-worth. Your dreams. Write them all. Honor them.

3. Speak the Reclamation

Read your list aloud. Then, say: *"I call every piece of me back home. I am not lost. I am returning."*

4. Dip Your Fingers in Water

Touch your forehead, heart, and hands with the water.

Say: *"I cleanse the lie that I had to lose myself to be loved. I am whole. I am mine."*

5. Mirror Invocation

Look into your eyes. Whisper: *"I will never abandon you again."*

6. Close in Stillness

Sit for three breaths. Let the silence wrap around you. Let your own presence be enough

Chapter 13:

Dancing with the Ghosts

Healing from the Betrayal That Changed Everything

There's a moment after betrayal that no one prepares you for. It's not the moment you find out. Not the moment you scream, break down, or beg for answers.

It's the quiet after when the world keeps spinning. When the groceries still need to be bought. When your children still need to be fed. When your heart still bleeds silently inside your chest while you smile politely at strangers.

It's the hollow dance with the ghosts of what once was and what you thought would always be.

You Wake Up Every Day Inside a War Zone

Every morning is a minefield. One step and you're fine. Another step and you're right back inside the night you discovered the messages, the lies, the betrayal.

You smile through breakfast. You tuck your pain into your pockets as you walk through your day. But it leaks anyway. It always leaks out of your eyes, your voice, your trembling hands.

No one tells you that betrayal changes the way you move through the world. No one tells you that even when the apology comes, even if the begging and promises pour in, you can still feel utterly, completely abandoned.

Because it wasn't just about another woman, it was about the lie you lived inside without knowing it. It was about loving someone who was living a double life behind your back. It was about realizing that love, no matter how fierce, doesn't always protect you.

You start to question your judgment. You replay conversations endlessly, trying to pinpoint the exact moment you became blind. You scrutinize every memory, every smile, every kiss, searching for the cracks you missed. You spiral through endless scenarios of *"what if"* and *"if only,"* torturing yourself with possibilities that will never change reality.

Sometimes, you find yourself talking to objects. The shampoo bottle, your car keys, even the microwave. You say things like, *"Can you believe this?"* like they were your emotional support group. In a twisted way, it's comforting. Because those things never lie to you.

The Battle Inside You

Part of you still wants to believe him. Part of you still wants to climb back into the fairy tale, even if you know the pages are torn and stained with betrayal.

You tell yourself: *"Maybe if I love harder, he'll stay this time." "Maybe if I'm prettier, sexier, thinner, sweeter... he won't need anyone else." "Maybe if I forgive fast enough, deep enough, completely enough ... it'll erase what he did."*

But deep down you know: You could turn yourself inside out and it would never change the choices he made in the dark.

You didn't fail. You didn't cause this. You didn't deserve it. But now you're the one carrying the wreckage. Now you're the one trying to stitch your heart back together with trembling fingers while pretending you're okay.

The Ghosts That Haunt You

It's not just him you're trying to heal from. It's her. It's them. It's the pictures you imagine in your mind of what he said, what he did, what he whispered in someone else's ear when he should have been coming home to you.

It's the version of him that belonged only to you and the version of him you can never unknow now. It's the way your mind betrays you, even when he's holding you at night, whispering that he loves you. It's the question that never stops burning: *"If he really loved me... how could he?"*

These ghosts don't vanish easily. They follow you through every conversation, every argument, every moment of intimacy. They whisper doubts in your ear at night. They replay your deepest insecurities like an endless, cruel movie. They are relentless.

Eventually, you start naming them. Ghost of Gaslighting. Phantom of Excuses. Lady of the Late-Night Texts. If you're going to dance with ghosts, you might as well know who you're tangoing with.

The Courage to Choose Yourself

Here's the hardest truth of all: Healing is not about erasing the betrayal. It's about deciding that you are worthy of more, no matter what he chooses.

You may stay. You may leave. But either way, you must make this vow to your battered, beautiful soul: *"I will not abandon myself in the name of saving someone else."*

You will not keep throwing yourself into the fire to keep someone else warm. You will not bleed out daily trying to stitch back together a dream he tore apart. You may still love him. But you must love yourself more.

The Rising

Healing will feel impossible sometimes. Some days you will sob in the shower. Some nights you will stare at the ceiling, aching for the version of your life that died when the betrayal was born.

But listen, please listen: You are not weak for hurting. You are not foolish for loving. You are not broken beyond repair. You are standing in the ashes of what was, barefoot and trembling, but you are still standing. And slowly, so slowly, you barely notice, you will begin to rise.

Maybe not in leaps. Maybe not even in full steps. But in heartbeats. In breaths. In small, sacred choices to love yourself even when everything inside you wants to give up.

You begin rising by setting boundaries that feel foreign and frightening at first. You begin rising by speaking truths that shake your voice but steady your soul. You rise by reclaiming spaces inside yourself you thought he had taken forever. You rise by reclaiming your laughter, your dreams, your peace.

Dancing with Ghosts

In time, these ghosts become less terrifying. They no longer hold you hostage. Instead, they remind you of your resilience, of your capacity to love fiercely, even after being deeply wounded. They teach you about the strength it takes to survive the unthinkable and to continue believing in your own worth.

Healing means recognizing these ghosts as witnesses, not judges. They remind you of where you've been, not where you must remain. You learn to dance with them, understanding they are part of your story but not your whole story.

You are the miracle. You are the phoenix. And even if you don't believe it... You are already beginning again.

You are already transforming pain into strength, betrayal into wisdom, heartbreak into hope. This dance is yours, raw and real, and undeniably brave. Embrace it. Own it. And trust that one day, your feet will know the steps to freedom by heart.

Closing Whispers

- I am allowed to mourn what I thought we had.

- I can hold grief in one hand and hope in the other.

- My wholeness was never dependent on someone else's honesty.

- I choose to rise, even in pieces.

- I am not defined by the lies told to me. I am defined by the truth I choose to live.

Soul Reflections

Questions to Sink Into

What ghosts am I still dancing with?

_____
_____
_____
_____
_____
_____
_____

What parts of myself need to be reclaimed, piece by piece?

_____
_____
_____
_____
_____
_____
_____

If I stopped trying to fix the broken pieces of him, what would I finally be free to heal in me?

_____
_____
_____
_____
_____
_____
_____

How can I love myself through the nights when no one else seems to know how?

_____
_____
_____
_____
_____
_____
_____

Sacred Mantra

"I will grieve what was. I will honor what I survived. I will become everything betrayal tried to destroy."

Healing Ritual: Ghost to Grace

1. **Set the Scene:** Light a white candle and dim the lights. Place a mirror in front of you.

2. *Call the Ghosts:* Say out loud the things that haunt you: *"I call forth the ghost of the lie," "the ghost of my doubt," "the ghost of what I lost."*

3. **Acknowledge and Release:** Write each ghost on a piece of paper. One by one, burn them safely (in a bowl or sink), saying: *"You no longer own me. I release you."*

4. *Reclaim the Space:* Look in the mirror. Place your hand on your heart and say: *"This is mine. My love, my truth, my becoming."*

5. **Dance it Out:** Play a song that makes you feel powerful. Let your body move. This is your celebration. You have survived the haunting. You are dancing your way into grace.

Chapter 14:

The Art of Rebuilding Yourself After Betrayal

There is a strange silence after heartbreak, a heavy quietness that blankets your life after the storm has passed. You wake up to the wreckage. The person you loved is still there or maybe they aren't, but either way, you realize the life you thought you were living no longer exists.

You are standing alone inside a life that looks like yours but feels like a stranger's.

The Shattered Mirror

After betrayal, your reflection changes. You don't just see your face anymore. You see the war you survived. You see the blood under your fingernails from clawing your way out of despair. You see the hollowed-out version of yourself staring back, blinking through the pain, asking: *"Who am I now?" "Where do I even begin to put myself back together?"*

The truth no one tells you is this: You can never rebuild the same life you had before. You are not the same woman. And that's not a curse, it's a sacred rebirth.

You might catch glimpses of her, in the way you brush your hair, in the songs that still make you cry, in the small, familiar rituals that feel both comforting and foreign. But she is no longer the woman you are becoming.

What shattered you also awakened you. The woman in the mirror is being reassembled not from the fragments of who you were, but from the raw truth of who you really are.

And that truth? She no longer apologizes for taking up space.

She doesn't shrink herself to make others comfortable. She doesn't tiptoe around people who handed her heartbreak and then expected a thank-you card. She builds altars out of broken pieces and calls them home.

The Loss of the Old You

You mourn her—the woman you were before the betrayal. You grieve her innocence. You grieve her trust. You grieve the woman who believed love was enough to protect her.

It's okay to miss her. It's okay to cry for her. It's okay to feel angry at the world for forcing you to become someone new without your consent. But here, in this place of ashes and emptiness, something remarkable begins: You get to choose who you become now. Not who he needs you to be. Not who the world expects you to be.

But who your soul has been aching for you to become all along.

This is the shedding of false skins. This is the reclamation of your power. This is where you stop asking for permission to exist fully and start living as though your truth is sacred. Because it is.

Rebuilding Isn't Linear

There will be days you feel strong and powerful, and then days you sob over an old text or a memory that sneaks up and sucker-punches you when you're just trying to eat your damn cereal. That's not failure. That's healing.

Healing is a dance between strength and sorrow. It is a sacred spiral, not a straight line. You will move forward. You will fall back. You will rage. You will forgive. You will grieve. You will hope.

All of it is part of the rising.

And yes, some days you'll feel like Beyoncé. Other days, like a leftover sock under the bed. Still rising. Progress will not always look like joy. Sometimes, it will look like simply not collapsing. Sometimes, it will look like breathing through a trigger instead of being swallowed by it.

Sometimes, healing is the quiet refusal to disappear.

The Small, Holy Steps

Healing doesn't come from giant, sweeping changes. It comes from tiny, almost invisible choices you make every day:

- Choosing to get out of bed even when it feels like your heart is too heavy to carry.

- Choosing to feed yourself even when you'd rather starve your way through the pain.

- Choosing to say no to the late-night spirals of self-blame.

- Choosing to breathe through the ache instead of drowning in it.

Every choice you make to choose life, even if life still feels hollow, is a stitch in the rebuilding of your soul. And some days, those stitches will unravel. That's okay. You start again.

You thread the needle of compassion through the fabric of your pain, and you sew yourself back together, again and again and again. You are not rebuilding your life for anyone else. You are rebuilding it for the woman in the mirror who refuses to give up.

You Are Not a Victim of Betrayal, You Are a Survivor of It

There is such brutal beauty in surviving the thing that tried to destroy you. Yes, betrayal cracked you wide open. Yes, it tore your world apart.

But inside the wreckage, there is soil rich enough to grow a new life, a life rooted in radical self-love, fierce boundaries, and a soul so luminous that no man, no betrayal, no loss could ever dim it again.

You are not doomed to stay broken. You are being remade into a woman who cannot be undone. This is your renaissance. This is your divine becoming.

You are rising not in spite of your scars, but because of them. You are becoming a lighthouse, not because you were never shipwrecked, but because you learned to shine through the darkest storms.

Closing Whispers

Whisper this into the bones of your spirit: "I am not who I was before the betrayal. I am not who they thought I would be. I am becoming someone they never saw coming."

Let the ghosts of the old you rest. She did her best with the tools she had. Now, it's time to build with fire in your veins and truth in your heart.

You don't have to rise gracefully. You just have to rise.

Soul Reflections

Questions to Sink Into

Who am I becoming through this heartbreak?

_____

_____

_____

_____

_____
_____
_____
_____

What pieces of myself am I reclaiming from the wreckage?

_____
_____
_____
_____
_____
_____
_____

What new foundations do I want to build my life upon now?

_____
_____
_____
_____
_____
_____
_____

How can I honor both my grief and my becoming without shame?

_____
_____
_____
_____
_____
_____
_____

Sacred Mantra

"I am not who I was before betrayal. I am becoming who I was always meant to be."

Healing Ritual: The Mirror & The Matchstick

You'll Need:

- A small mirror

- A piece of paper

- A pen

- A match or lighter

- A safe bowl or fireproof dish

Steps:

1. Sit in front of the mirror. Look at yourself, really look. Let the tears come. Let the anger rise. Say her name: *"I see you."*

2. Write down everything you were taught to be … the pleaser, the forgiver, the fixer, the woman who stayed silent.

3. Fold the paper. Hold it in your hand and whisper: *"I release what was never mine to carry. I return these roles to the fire."*

4. Light the paper safely and watch it burn. As the smoke rises, say: *"I reclaim myself. Piece by piece. Flame by flame."*

5. Blow a kiss to your reflection. You're not broken. You are becoming.

Chapter 15:

Reclaiming the Pieces They Couldn't Steal

There comes a moment, soft and sharp at the same time, where you realize something sacred: They broke parts of you... but they didn't break you. The pieces they shattered were never the whole story.

The love you gave so freely, the dreams you built around their promises, the loyalty you offered like a lifeline, those things were real. They came from the deepest, most holy place inside you. And they were never dependent on someone else's ability to treasure them.

This truth hits differently. Not like lightning. Not with rage. But with the solemn quiet of finally seeing clearly. It comes after the chaos dies down, when you are sitting alone in the aftermath, wrapped in your own aching silence.

And yet, beneath all the sorrow, there is a strange flicker of something sacred: knowing they never had the power to take everything. Knowing they only touched the surface.

And let's be real …for a while, you might have felt like everything was gone. Like the last good parts of you got packed up in their emotional U-Haul and driven off into the sunset. But healing whispers something bold: They never really knew what they had… and thank God, they never got close enough to steal what matters most.

What Betrayal Couldn't Touch

He took your trust and crumpled it in his hands. He took your dreams and dragged them through the mud. He took your laughter, your bright shining eyes, and made them dim for a while.

But listen to me:

- He could not take your soul's fire.

- He could not take your capacity to love.

- He could not take the wild, sacred woman inside you who knows her worth even when the world tries to convince her otherwise.

Let's pause and honor that. Because betrayal may have knocked you down, bloodied your spirit, and made you question your sanity, but it did not steal the core of who you are. That core, bruised maybe, battered certainly… is still burning. Waiting. Calling you back home to yourself.

Sure, some days you might feel more like a hot mess than a holy reclamation, crying into your coffee, Googling *"How to erase a man from your nervous system,"* and wondering if emotional lobotomies are a thing. But even on those days, even in those spirals, you're still here. Still healing. Still unbroken in the ways that matter. And honestly? If a playlist of '90s breakup ballads, some carbs, and a rage-cleaning session is what gets you through, so be it. That's not regression. That's survival with style.

The Myth of "Lost" Pieces

You are not broken in ways that cannot be repaired. You are not ruined. You are not some tragic figure destined to limp through life with a shattered heart. You are a masterpiece still in the making.

And let me be blunt: This isn't a Hallmark card. This is your real, raw, blood-and-bones truth. Every piece of you that felt lost after betrayal is still there, buried under the rubble, perhaps, but never destroyed.

And now is the time to dig your hands into the ash and the wreckage and begin pulling them back into the light:

- Your laughter.

- Your sensuality.

- Your dreams.

- Your fierceness.

- Your deep, oceanic love for life itself.

None of it was lost. It was hidden. It was waiting for you to choose yourself again. And no, you don't have to *"bounce back"* in some glorious Instagram-worthy glow-up with matching affirmation tattoos and green juice in hand. Sometimes reclaiming yourself looks more like crying in the bathtub one night and laughing at a dumb meme the next morning.

Both are sacred. Both are proof that you're still in here, still fighting for yourself in ways no one sees.

The Wild Reclamation

Reclaiming yourself after betrayal isn't soft. It's wild. It's furious. It's breathtaking.

It looks like:

- Saying no to the guilt they tried to lay on your shoulders.

- Saying yes to your right to be loved with reverence and loyalty.

- Taking your body back as something sacred not something abandoned.

- Choosing your happiness without asking for permission.

And yes, it also looks like finally deleting their number… for the sixth time… and not re-saving it the next time you're wine-sad and nostalgic. Because girl, we've all been there.

It's looking at the mirror with tear-stained cheeks and whispering: *"I am still worthy. I am still beautiful. I am still me, maybe even more than before."*

This reclamation isn't about pretending it didn't hurt. It's about honoring how deeply it hurt and still deciding that you are bigger than the pain. It's about being the warrior who rose from her own ashes and crowned herself. And it's also about softness. About grace. About holding yourself with tenderness on the days you feel like slipping back into sorrow.

Reclamation isn't a constant roar…sometimes, it's a whisper that says, *"I'll try again today."*

The First Step Back to Yourself

You don't have to have it all figured out. You don't have to know who you are becoming. You don't have to rebuild everything overnight. You just have to take one small step back toward yourself.

Maybe today, that step is:

- Forgiving yourself for staying too long.

- Letting go of the question *"why wasn't I enough?"*

- Breathing deeply when the sadness hits, instead of drowning.

- Dancing in your kitchen barefoot even though you feel hollow.

Small steps. Sacred steps. Powerful steps. Maybe tomorrow the step looks like journaling your rage. Maybe next week, it looks like saying no to someone who drains you. Maybe it's choosing solitude over begging to be seen.

All of these are steps back home, back to the soul of who you truly are. You don't need to be graceful or polished or Pinterest-worthy while you do it. You just need to keep going.

And if your mascara's running and your house is a mess and your heart feels like a battlefield, so be it. That's still a woman rising.

Closing Whispers

Whisper this into your palms when they tremble, into your chest when it aches:

"They never held the best parts of me because those parts were always mine."

You didn't lose your power. You just stopped recognizing it for a while. But now? Now you remember. And nothing is more dangerous to those who betrayed you than a woman who has reclaimed herself.

Soul Reflections

Questions to Sink Into

What parts of me feel buried beneath the pain, and how can I begin to reclaim them?

_____

_____

_____
_____
_____
_____
_____

What did betrayal not take from me, no matter how it tried?

_____
_____
_____
_____
_____
_____
_____

What small, wild act of rebellion (of self-love) can I gift myself today?

_____
_____
_____
_____
_____
_____
_____

Sacred Mantra

"I reclaim the pieces they could not steal. I rise from the ashes of betrayal; burning brighter, loving fiercer, living freer."

Healing Ritual: The Ashes & The Altar

This ritual is a reclamation, a soulful gathering of the parts of you that were scattered by betrayal. Begin by collecting a few sacred items: a candle in any color that makes you feel powerful, a small dish of salt or ash to symbolize purification and transformation, a pen and paper, and a song that reminds you of who you were before the pain…that wild, radiant version of you who danced through life before she was wounded.

Light the candle, and as the flame rises, speak these words aloud with intention: *"I am reclaiming what was always mine."* Let the light bear witness to your return. Then take your paper and begin writing a list of everything you feel was stolen from you… your laughter, your confidence, your voice, your dreams, your joy. Name each one. Call it out of hiding.

Now, one by one, speak each item over the flame. For example: *"My voice returns to me now. I call it back."* Let the words be a spell, a declaration, a sacred vow. After each reclaiming, take a small pinch of the salt or ash and place it in your hand. This is your altar, not on a table, but in your palm, symbolizing that everything you are reclaiming lives within you now.

When your list is complete, place your hand over your heart. Feel the weight of that altar, not heavy, but grounding. Then play your chosen song. Let it awaken the part of you that remembers. Cry if you need to. Dance. Scream. Laugh. Whatever your soul needs, give her that release. Let it move through you, let it rise. And when you're ready, close the ritual by declaring: *"I am whole. I am wild. I am free. And I am mine again."*

This is your return. Welcome home.

Chapter 16:

Forgiving the Woman in the Mirror

You stand there, staring at yourself, and you barely recognize the woman looking back. The deep sadness around your eyes. The tension in your jaw. The way your shoulders slump, carrying more weight than they were ever meant to bear.

You think:

"How did I end up here?"

"Why wasn't I enough to make him stay?"

"Why didn't I see the signs?"

"Why did I believe in him, in us, for so long?" The shame seeps in quietly at first... then it becomes deafening. And you realize: It's not just him you're angry at. It's yourself.

The Silent Guilt That Betrayal Leaves Behind

We talk so much about forgiving others but no one tells you how brutal it is to forgive yourself.

To forgive yourself for:

- Loving someone who didn't know how to love you back.

- Believing promises that turned into broken glass.

- Staying when maybe you should have left.

- Hoping against all odds that things would change.

- Losing pieces of yourself along the way.

The betrayal cuts you once. Your own blame and self-hate cut you a thousand times more. And if you're not careful, you'll end up punishing yourself far longer than he ever could. Because here's the twisted part: Self-blame feels like control. If it was your fault, then maybe next time, you can fix it. Be smarter. Love less. Guard more. Don't trust anyone.

But that's not healing, that's self-imprisonment with prettier wallpaper. And let's not pretend this isn't messy. One minute you're vowing to let go and love yourself, the next you're Googling, *"Was it really my fault?"* at 3 AM while eating peanut butter out of the jar with a spoon.

Healing isn't linear; it's chaotic, sweaty, ugly-crying work. But it's also holy. And sometimes, honestly? It's also weird. Like finding yourself talking out loud to your cat about emotional boundaries and realizing she's the best listener you've had all week.

You Were Never the Villain

Listen to me: You were never foolish for loving. You were never weak in trusting. You were never wrong for wanting to believe in someone you chose to give your heart to. Your love was not the mistake. His betrayal was. There's a world of difference. You didn't ruin the relationship by loving him too much.

He ruined it by not being someone capable of holding the love you offered. The world will try to tell you:

"You should have known."

"You should have left sooner."

"You made it easy for him."

But here's the truth no one shouts loud enough: It is never your fault when someone chooses to betray you. It is never your fault that you loved with your whole heart. There is no shame in being a woman who believes in love. There is no shame in being someone who stayed loyal while someone else played games with your soul.

So let them judge. Let the peanut gallery gossip. Let your auntie at Thanksgiving side-eye you with that *"I told you so"* tone. None of them knows the whole truth. None of them had to survive what you did. And none of them are qualified to write your redemption story. (Also, let's be honest, Aunt Sheila still cries over her high school boyfriend from 1983. Glass houses, Sheila.)

The Hardest Apology You'll Ever Make

You need to sit with yourself, with the woman trembling inside you, and whisper what no one else ever says: *"I'm sorry I blamed you. I'm sorry I made you carry this shame. I'm sorry I punished you for loving so deeply."*

You need to apologize to the girl who fell headfirst into hope. The one who dreamed of forever. The one who believed in promises. You need to be the one who finally says to her:

"You did nothing wrong by wanting more."

"You are not stupid, naive, or weak."

"You are powerful beyond measure because you loved even when you were hurt."

And if that feels awkward, if you feel like a total cheeseball talking to your reflection, lean into it. Speak anyway. Speak kindly. Speak honestly. Speak until the woman in the mirror starts to feel like an ally instead of a stranger.

Because that girl you're blaming? She got you through. She kept breathing when it would have been easier to stop. She held on when no one else showed up. She deserves your love, not your punishment.

The Brave Act of Loving Yourself Again

Forgiving yourself looks like:

- Holding yourself tenderly when the grief washes over you at 2 AM.

- Speaking to yourself with the same compassion you would give your best friend.

- Choosing not to let your past determine your worth.

- Giving yourself permission to heal at your own pace.

It looks like choosing yourself even when you feel most unlovable. It looks like being your own savior when no one else shows up. It looks like deciding that you are worthy of love, respect, and joy starting with how you treat yourself.

And sometimes? Loving yourself looks like blocking his number. Again. For the fourth time. And not unblocking it this time just because Mercury is in retrograde and you're feeling nostalgic.

Forgiveness isn't a one-time event. It's a thousand small acts of kindness toward the woman you are and the woman you are becoming. It's messy. It's painful. It's liberating. And it is your birthright.

It's also allowed to be funny sometimes. Like laughing mid-cry because you realize you're still wearing your ex's hoodie while journaling about releasing the past. (Yes. That happened. And yes. We burn the hoodie after.)

You Are Worth Forgiving

You were never too broken. You were never too foolish. You were never too trusting. You were human. You were love in its purest form. And now even with the scars you are still that woman. Braver. Softer. Wiser. And ready, finally, to come home to yourself.

So, look in that mirror. Raise your chin. Smile, even if your eyes are still wet. And say, *"I'm not perfect. But I'm still here. And I'm still sacred."*

Because you are. And you always were.

Closing Whispers

Speak this slowly, like a love letter to your own heart: *"I forgive the girl who didn't know better. I honor the woman who survived anyway. And I vow to never abandon myself again, not for love, not for loyalty, not for anyone."*

Soul Reflections

Questions to Sink Into

What harsh words have I spoken to myself about this betrayal?

_____

_____

_____

_____

_____

_____

How have I punished myself unfairly for someone else's choices?

_____
_____
_____
_____
_____
_____
_____

What would it feel like to start forgiving myself, piece by piece?

_____
_____
_____
_____
_____
_____
_____

Sacred Mantra

"I forgive the woman in the mirror. I honor the love she gave. I choose to love her more fiercely than ever before."

Healing Ritual: The Mirror and the Flame

You'll Need:

- A handheld or standing mirror

- A candle

- A quiet space

- A photo of yourself from a time when you were happiest (optional)

Steps:

1. Light the candle and sit comfortably in front of the mirror.

2. Gaze at your own reflection. Not to critique. Not to inspect. Just to see.

3. Place your hand over your heart and softly speak these words: *"I forgive you. I see your pain. I honor your strength. I love who you are becoming."*

4. If using a photo of your younger self, hold it gently and say: *"Thank you for getting me here. I've got us now."*

5. Let the candle burn while you breathe deeply. Let the silence be the ceremony. Let the forgiveness settle in.

6. Close with: *"I choose me. Today. Tomorrow. Always."*

Chapter 17:

Rising from the Ashes

There is a moment after the heartbreak, after the betrayal, after the endless nights of crying into your pillow, where something shifts. It's almost imperceptible at first, like a single flicker of light in a pitch-black room. But it's there.

Hope.

Not the reckless, naïve kind of hope you had before, the one that believed people would never hurt you. No, this is a wiser hope. A weathered, defiant hope. Hope that has survived the inferno and still whispers, *"There's more to your story than this."* Hope that stretches out a trembling hand and says, *"Come on, beautiful soul. Get up. We're not done yet."*

You realize something earth-shattering: You didn't die. Your heart broke into a thousand unrecognizable pieces. Your world as you knew it crumbled around you. You grieved a life you thought you'd live.

And yet... You. Are. Still. Here.

Your heart still beats. Your soul still sings, even if right now, it's a whisper. And that means your story isn't over. Not even close.

The Ashes You Stand In

Everything familiar feels like ashes now. The dreams you held so tightly have slipped through your fingers like dust. The laughter that once wrapped itself around your home now echoes like a haunting.

The promises made in soft whispers feel like cruel betrayals. You are standing in the remnants of what was. You are standing in the heavy silence of things left unsaid. You are standing in the rubble of a life you loved fiercely and lost painfully.

And let's not sugarcoat it: this is not the *"beautiful mess"* Instagram posts romanticize. This is ugly-crying-into-your-laundry-pile, doom-scrolling your text thread at midnight, and wondering how you ever thought this was love. This is heartbreak in its rawest, messiest, most human form.

It's tempting to crumble with it. To kneel down and say, *"I can't rebuild. It's too much. I'm too broken."* But listen, the ashes you stand in? They aren't just death. They are also soil.

The soil of rebirth. The place where seeds crack open and green shoots defy the death around them. This is your beginning. Right here, in the mess. Right here, in the ruin. Not because you wanted it. But because you are worthy of more than what shattered you.

And don't worry if you're not feeling particularly *"phoenix-y"* right now. You don't need to rise with glitter and grace. You can crawl, cuss, cry, and still rise. Ashes are messy, and so is rebirth. You can have bedhead, chipped nail polish, and a heart that still stings… and you can still be rising.

Becoming Someone New

There is no going back. There is no returning to the innocent girl who trusted without fear. And maybe, maybe that's a gift. Because now you are becoming a woman who knows her worth like she knows her own heartbeat. You are becoming a woman who no longer begs to be loved but demands to be respected. You are becoming a woman who sets herself on fire for no one but lights up her own damn sky.

You are building a life that no one can take from you. A joy that no betrayal can steal. A peace that no lie can disturb. You are no longer waiting to be chosen. You are choosing yourself. Every day. Every time. Without apology.

Let's be real: Waiting for someone else to save you is exhausting.

And spoiler alert, they're not coming. The plot twist? You were always your own salvation. You were always your own miracle.

You didn't need to be rescued. You just needed to remember you had wings. Now it's time to live like it.

The Sacred Rebirth

If you could see your soul right now, you wouldn't recognize the fierce beauty emerging from your pain. Your wings, once tattered, are being reforged in fire. Your heart, once cracked, is healing stronger, softer, and wilder.

You are a phoenix, my love. You were always meant to burn down what no longer served you, to rise untouched by the chains that once held you.

And your rising? It will be breathtaking.

You will laugh again, not because life is perfect, but because you are finally free. You will love again, not because you are desperate, but because you are abundant. You will dream again, not because you are foolish, but because you are brave beyond belief.

And let's pause and say this out loud: Your best days are not behind you. They are ahead of you, shimmering just beyond the horizon. You may not see them clearly yet. You may still be limping, still healing, still aching. But you are moving.

And every step you take toward healing is a declaration: *"I will not be defined by what broke me. I will be defined by how beautifully I rose."* And When It Doesn't Feel Like Rising…

Some days you won't feel like a phoenix. You'll feel like roadkill with mascara. You'll feel like you're drowning in your own bed sheets, clutching a heating pad, and crying into last week's pizza.

And that's okay. That's part of it, too.

Rising doesn't always look like flight. Sometimes it looks like crawling with bloody knees and a shaky voice saying, *"I'm not done yet."*

So, on those days, be gentle. Don't demand strength, just softness. Just presence. Just one breath. One tiny step forward.

That's still rising.

Your Rise is Inevitable

There's a version of you not far from now who is dancing barefoot in a kitchen she loves, laughing at something silly, her heart light again.

She doesn't flinch at his name. She doesn't question her worth. She doesn't apologize for her strength. She knows she is whole. She knows she is holy. She knows the fire didn't destroy her; it refined her.

And that version of you? She's waiting for you. She's calling you.

She's already lighting the path back home. So, rise, love.

Messy. Unapologetically. Fiercely. Ashes and all.

Closing Whispers

Lean in, love. These are for your soul.

- You are allowed to mourn and still move.

- You are allowed to weep and still rise.

- You are allowed to be both broken and beautiful at the same time.

- You are not behind. You are becoming.

- You do not need anyone else to choose you. You have already been chosen by the divine within.

- Let this be the moment you say: *"I am mine before I am anyone else's."*

You are not the ruins. You are the rebuilder. You are not the heartbreak. You are the healing.

Soul Reflections

Questions to Sink Into

What parts of my old life and identity are ready to be burned away?

_____
_____
_____
_____
_____
_____
_____

What new strengths have already begun growing inside me, even through the pain?

_____
_____
_____
_____
_____
_____
_____

How would I live differently if I believed my best days were still coming?

_____
_____
_____
_____
_____
_____

What would it feel like to choose joy again, not because life is perfect, but because I deserve it?

_____
_____
_____
_____
_____
_____

Sacred Mantra

"From these ashes, I am reborn. From this heartbreak, I rise stronger. From this ending, I create my beginning."

Healing Ritual: Ashes to Embers

You'll need:

- A small candle (any color, but red or white symbolizes rebirth)

- A bowl of water

- A mirror

- A piece of paper and a pen

Steps:

1. Light the Candle

As you light the candle, say aloud: *"From these ashes, I rise. I am not broken. I am becoming."*

2. Look in the Mirror

Stare into your own eyes even if they're puffy or tired or rimmed with tears.

Say out loud: *"You didn't deserve the pain, but you deserve the healing. I forgive you. I love you. I choose you."*

3. Write It Down

Write a letter that starts with: *"To the woman I am becoming…"*

Let it pour out. The grief. The hope. The sacred truth.

4. Water Blessing

Dip your fingers into the bowl of water. Gently press them to your heart.

Say: *"I baptize myself in my own truth. I cleanse myself of what was. I rise into what will be."*

5. Close with Flame

Blow out the candle and whisper: *"This is not the end. This is the awakening."*

Let it be the beginning of everything beautiful.

Chapter 18:

Choosing Yourself, Again and Again

There comes a moment after the storm when the tears dry, the heart scars over, and the world stops spinning, when you are left with one question: Will I choose myself?

Because healing isn't just about surviving heartbreak, it isn't just about patching up the broken pieces. It's about choosing actively, daily, fiercely to love yourself enough never to settle again. It's about standing at the crossroads of fear and freedom and deciding that your life, your peace, your soul are too precious to sacrifice for half-hearted love. It's about looking in the mirror and whispering: *"I choose you even when no one else did. Even when they left. Even when you doubted yourself, I choose you."*

And some days? That whisper might sound more like a war cry. Other days, it might sound like *"Okay, girl, let's just not text him back today, we'll call that growth."* Both counts. Both matters.

The Truth About Healing

They don't tell you this, but healing doesn't always feel magical. It doesn't always feel empowering. Some days it feels like dragging yourself through mud. Some days it feels like sobbing on the bathroom floor again, even when you thought you were *"over it."* Some days it feels like smiling on the outside but feeling hollow inside.

Healing can look like crying in the Target parking lot while holding a rotisserie chicken. Healing can sound like blasting breakup anthems at full volume and screaming along in your car. Healing is ugly, sacred work. But here's the sacred truth you must hold onto: You are still healing even on the days it feels like you're falling apart.

Healing isn't linear. It spirals. It dips. It rages. It tests every ounce of strength you didn't know you had. It will pull you under, then bring you back to shore again. But every single time you choose yourself, even in the smallest way, you are winning.

Every time you say, *"I deserve peace more than I deserve to hold onto this pain,"* you are becoming more unstoppable. Every time you walk away from people who treat you like you're disposable, you are rewriting your story. Every time you set a boundary, speak your truth, say *"no,"* say *"yes,"* love yourself more fiercely than anyone else ever has, you are rising.

And if anyone makes you feel guilty for that, feel free to mail them a glitter bomb of boundaries with a note that says, *"Respectfully, I'm busy saving my own damn life."*

Choosing Yourself Doesn't Mean You're Selfish

It means you finally understood what they didn't… that your soul is not up for negotiation. That you are not here to be loved halfway. That you were not made to beg for scraps of affection. That your heart was meant to be celebrated, not tolerated.

Choosing yourself is not a betrayal of anyone else; it's the most sacred vow you can make. *"I vow to protect the girl inside me who was hurt. I vow to honor the woman I am becoming. I vow to never again abandon myself for the comfort of others."*

You aren't selfish for wanting a full life. You aren't selfish for demanding respect. You aren't selfish for walking away from people who cannot meet you at the level of your healing.

You are sovereign. You are sacred. You are your own salvation.

And if someone calls you *"too much"* for that? Good. Be too much. Be overflowing. Be untouchable. Be exactly the kind of woman who scares people who rely on your self-abandonment.

It Is Safe to Trust Yourself Again

Maybe the betrayals taught you to doubt your instincts. Maybe the lies made you question your reality. Maybe the broken promises hollowed out your ability to believe.

But the more profound truth is, your soul has never stopped speaking to you. Every gut feeling, every whisper of intuition, every little tug inside your chest, it has all been your soul trying to guide you home.

And now, you get to listen again. Now, you get to trust that voice. Now, you get to rebuild a relationship with yourself stronger than any bond with anyone else.

You are not crazy. You are not *"too much."* You are not unworthy. You are intuitive. You are wise. You are divinely guided.

You have always known the way, even when you were scared to walk it. And now you're brave enough to take the first steps. You're not just rebuilding. You're becoming untouchable. Unapologetic. Unmistakably aligned.

This isn't about revenge. It's about reclamation.

The Art of Choosing Yourself, Again and Again

Choosing yourself once is brave. Choosing yourself every day is revolutionary.

On the days when old wounds whisper lies, choose yourself. On the days when loneliness feels heavier than the healing, choose yourself. On the days when memories try to seduce you back into pain, choose yourself. On the days when hope feels like a fragile, reckless thing, choose yourself.

Even if you have to choose yourself through tears. Even if you have to choose yourself through shaking hands. Even if choosing yourself means walking away from everything you once thought would be your forever. Not because it's easy. Not because it's perfect. But because your future is worth the fight.

Because the life that's waiting for you, the love that's waiting for you, the peace, the abundance, the joy, all of it begins with the sacred, radical act of saying: *"I choose me." "I choose my healing." "I choose my freedom." "I choose my soul."*

And when you do, the universe rearranges itself to meet you there. And if no one claps for you? Clap for your damn self. Light a candle. Dance alone in your kitchen. Toast your becoming.

You're doing the bravest thing a woman can do, refusing to betray herself ever again.

Closing Whispers

You were never too broken to be whole again. You were never too lost to be found. You were never too hurt to be healed. Your story was never over. It was just waiting for you to make your choice.

And now you have.

So here is what I whisper over you now: You are the author and the altar. You are the healer and the healed. You are not a supporting role in someone else's life; you are the damn headline. You don't need approval; you need alignment. You are already enough. Always were. And the sacred woman within you? She's just getting started.

Soul Reflections

Questions to Sink Into

When was the last time I truly, unapologetically chose myself?

_____
_____
_____
_____
_____
_____
_____

What patterns have I repeated that kept me small, silent, or second?

_____
_____
_____
_____
_____
_____
_____

Who am I when I am not trying to earn love, prove worth, or fix others?

_____
_____
_____
_____
_____
_____
_____

What would my life look like if I honored my soul's truth every single day?

_____
_____
_____
_____
_____
_____
_____

What is one loving boundary I can set right now to protect my peace?

_____
_____
_____
_____
_____
_____
_____

Sacred Mantra

"I am the flame and the altar. I choose myself with holy conviction. I am no longer waiting, I am becoming."

Healing Ritual: "The Mirror & The Flame"

What You'll Need:

A small mirror. A candle and a lighter. A journal. A cozy space

Step 1: Light the Candle. Say aloud: _"I choose me. Even when it's hard. Especially when it's hard. I choose me."_

Step 2: Look in the Mirror Gaze into your own eyes, even if it's awkward. Especially if it's awkward, say: *"I forgive you. I believe you. I'm proud of you. I love you."*

Step 3: Journal Write a page beginning with: *"When I choose myself, I..."* Let your heart pour out.

Step 4: Breathe deeply. Place your hand over your heart. Feel it. That's yours. That's home. Say: *"This is the heartbeat of a woman who rises."*

Step 5: Blow out the candle. Say: *"It is done. I am chosen. I am whole."*

You are the miracle. You are the masterpiece. And from this moment on, you don't just survive. You rise.

Chapter 19:

The New Life After Healing

At first, you will barely notice it. It won't crash into your life like a thunderstorm or sweep you off your feet like a tidal wave. No, it will come softly, tenderly. A flicker. A single breath that doesn't ache.

A morning when you realize your first thought is not sorrow. It will be in the way your heart feels a little lighter when you hear your favorite song. It will be in the way the sunset catches your eye and you smile, truly smile, for the first time in what feels like forever.

This is how the new life begins. Quiet. Gentle. Unfolding in the spaces where grief once lived. At first, you won't trust it. You'll wonder if it's a trick, a temporary fluke, like a glitch in the system of your sadness. You'll brace yourself for the next wave, the next memory ambush, the next *"I miss him"* out of nowhere.

But then… it doesn't come. And in that stillness, you start to believe maybe this peace is real.

The Death That Births New Life

Healing is a death, yes. But it is also a sacred birth. You shed old versions of yourself, the ones built on survival, fear, and longing. You bury the woman who tolerated crumbs, who begged for love, who twisted herself into knots to be chosen.

You grieve her like a sister. You honor her for trying. But you do not drag her forward. And from that sacred burial, something breathtaking rises: A woman reborn from her own ashes. She walks differently. She speaks differently. She demands nothing but attracts everything meant for her, effortlessly. She doesn't chase anymore; she draws. She doesn't explain herself; she embodies herself.

You realize, finally, that the death was necessary. Because you were never meant to live half-alive, waiting for permission to be loved. You were meant to be wildly, fiercely alive, a force of nature all your own.

And yes, there will be days you still grieve her, the girl who stayed, the woman who tried. But now you also celebrate the woman who finally chose herself and burned it all down to begin again.

This is your resurrection. This is your return to power.

The Quiet Miracles of Healing

You may not recognize them at first, these tiny resurrections:

- The day you dance barefoot in your kitchen without worrying who's watching.

- The evening you laugh, not a brittle, polite laugh, but a soul-deep, belly laugh that feels like coming home.

- The moment you make a decision for yourself, unapologetically, freely, and don't second-guess it.

- The night you sleep deeply, without dreams of betrayal, without waking up gasping for air.

- The moment you realize you haven't thought about him in days… and don't even feel guilty.

These moments are small, yes. But they are sacred. They are the stitches weaving a new life together, one of self-trust, self-respect, and self-love.

And you will realize: *The life you were waiting for is already here.*

It's being built inside you, heartbeat by heartbeat. It isn't dramatic. It isn't cinematic. It's better. It's real. It's quiet mornings and peaceful thoughts. It's your own damn voice in your head, not his. And sometimes, it's as simple as this: realizing you didn't check your phone, hoping he'd text. That's healing, too.

You Were Always Enough

The cruelest lie heartbreak tells you is that you were somehow not enough. Let me rip that lie to shreds right now: You. Were. Always. Enough.

You are enough in the moments you ache. You are enough in the moments you rage. You are enough in the moments you rebuild. You are enough when you light up a room. You are enough when you can't get off the couch. You are not broken. You are becoming. You are not ruined. You are being remade.

Every scar, every shattered hope, every tear has been alchemized into a deeper, richer soul.

The woman rising from these ashes does not beg for love. She does not chase it. She embodies it. She radiates it. She walks into rooms carrying her own sunlight. She makes the ground tremble under the strength of her healed heart.

You are her. You always were. The only difference now is: you finally believe it.

What the New Life Feels Like

Imagine it:

- Peace so deep it anchors you even when chaos storms around you.

- Love so pure it starts from within you and spills out into the world.

- Freedom to live, love, and breathe without shackles of fear or shame.

- Joy that bubbles up unexpectedly, like a champagne glass overflowing with golden laughter.

- Purpose so powerful that even your quiet days feel sacred.

This is what your new life feels like. Not perfect. Not without hard days. But yours. Authentic. Bold. Untamed. Joyful. What things used to consume you? They shrink. The people who once defined your worth? They become irrelevant. The triggers that once shattered you? They soften into reminders of how far you've come.

You are not surviving anymore. You are thriving. And love? Oh, it will find you again, but it won't complete you. It will complement you. It will rise to meet the standard you now hold for your life, your soul, your heart.

Because now you know: You are already whole. You were never waiting to be completed. You were waiting to be seen by you.

The Dream Beyond the Pain

Beyond this heartbreak is a dream so beautiful it would take your breath away if you could glimpse it fully now.

- It's mornings where you wake up with a heart brimming with gratitude instead of grief.

- It's friendships rooted in soul connection, not obligation.

- It's love that feels like freedom, not chains.

- It's a relationship with yourself that is so tender, so fierce, so sacred, you never again allow anyone to violate your boundaries or dim your light.

This dream is not a fantasy. It is your destiny if you are brave enough to keep walking. And you are. You always have been. Every painful step you have taken has brought you closer to this, this radiant life that has been waiting patiently for you to claim it. So go claim it. Walk like you deserve it. Because you do.

But let's be honest, the new life doesn't always show up like a damn Hallmark movie. Some days it still sucks. Some days, you'll miss the chaos because at least it was familiar. Some days, you'll wonder if healing is just an expensive word for *"learning how to cry less in public."* And some days, you'll still instinctively reach for your phone to send a text... before remembering you've deleted his number (again).

This new life isn't about pretending the past didn't matter. It's about realizing you matter more. And if you find yourself rebuilding your life in sweatpants with mascara-streaked cheeks, surrounded by half-eaten chocolate and Amazon boxes filled with healing crystals and bath bombs? That's not failure, that's a rebirth in progress.

Because healing isn't always spa days and journaling, sometimes it's rage-cleaning your kitchen at 2 AM to break up playlists while yelling, "I CHOOSE ME, DAMN IT!" at your air fryer.

Sacred? Yes.

A mess? Also, yes.

But slowly... you'll catch glimpses of her, the woman you're becoming. And she'll be everything you once prayed for: Unapologetic. Untouchable. Unshakably at peace.

You won't even notice at first how powerful you've become. But then someone will try to cross a boundary you used to bend for… and you won't flinch. That's when you'll know: She's here. You're her. And you're not going back.

Closing Whispers

This is not a happy ending. This is a holy beginning. You didn't just survive the fire; you became it. And the woman who rises now? She doesn't beg. She doesn't explain. She doesn't settle. She knows. Knows that her softness is strength. Knows that her joy is sacred. Knows that her healing was never about him; it was always about her remembering who the hell she is.

So let the world stare. Let them wonder how you made it through. Smile. Fix your crown. Pour yourself a glass of champagne or tea or moon water, whatever your spirit craves, and toast to the most divine thing you've ever done:

You came home to yourself.

Soul Reflections

Questions to Sink Into

What are the small moments that signal my healing has taken root?

_____
_____
_____
_____
_____
_____
_____

Who is the woman I'm becoming, and how does she speak, move, and love?

_____
_____
_____
_____
_____
_____
_____

What grief am I still honoring, and what joy am I ready to receive?

_____
_____
_____
_____
_____
_____

Where do I still carry remnants of the old story?

_____
_____
_____
_____
_____
_____

How does my life begin to shift when I believe I'm already enough?

_____
_____

_____

_____

_____

_____

_____

Sacred Mantra

"I am the resurrection and the rise. I am the soft power of peace and the bold force of becoming. My healing is my homecoming. And I choose this life, wildly and without apology."

Healing Ritual: "The First Morning of Forever"

This ritual is for the moment when you're finally ready to rise, not just from the ashes, but into the life that was always meant for you. Begin by gathering a few simple items: a blank piece of paper or a journal, a candle, a glass of water, and a song that stirs something deep inside you, the kind that makes you feel alive in your bones.

When you're ready, light the candle and let the flame hold space for your rebirth. As it glows, say aloud with conviction: *"I release the story that was. I step into the life that's mine. I am no longer surviving, I am thriving."* Let those words echo through you like a promise made in firelight.

Next, take your pen and write a letter from your future, healed self, the version of you who's standing in her power, glowing, grounded, and free, and address it to the you who once begged for scraps of love. Begin the letter with: *"Thank you for surviving... here's what's waiting for us now."* Let it flow. Be as raw or sacred or funny as you need to be. Tell her what she made it through. Tell her what's coming. Remind her who the hell she is.

Then, pick up your glass of water. Hold it with both hands and speak your intention into it like a blessing: *"This is my new beginning. I choose life, joy, and peace."* Drink it slowly. Let it fill you. Let it baptize your insides with new truth.

Now, play the song. Let the music move you. Dance, sway, breathe deep, and smile even if your smile comes with tears. Let your body feel what freedom tastes like. Let yourself remember how it feels to be fully alive, even in the aftermath.

When you're ready to close the ritual, blow out the candle and whisper softly: *"I am here. I am whole. My new life has begun."*

And just like that, a new chapter is born. Welcome to your forever.

Chapter 20:

Thriving in Your Life

There is a morning after the longest night. A moment when the air feels different, lighter, as if the Universe itself is breathing life back into you. At first, you may not trust it. The ground may still feel a little shaky beneath your feet, like your legs don't quite know how to carry the weight of peace.

That's okay.

Healing isn't about forgetting the darkness. It's about learning to dance in the light despite the memory of the storms. You are awakening. You are remembering. You are becoming. And the sun that now rises before you is not the same sun from before. It is warmer, softer, gentler, and it shines only for you.

Learning to Trust Life Again

It's terrifying, isn't it? After heartbreak, betrayal, devastation, trusting life feels like the most dangerous thing you could ever do. You've built walls with your bare hands. You've made promises to yourself like, *"Never again will I be caught off guard." "Never again will I love so fully and be shattered for it."*

But here's the deeper truth: You didn't survive all of that to live half a life. You didn't battle through those sleepless nights, those soul-crushing days, to sit on the sidelines of your own existence. You were made for joy. You were made for wild laughter, for sunsets that make you cry with their beauty, for love so deep it feels like breathing.

Trust doesn't come all at once. It comes in small brave acts:

- Trusting the morning to bring you another chance.

- Trusting your own wisdom to protect you.

- Trusting that even if life hurts again, you are strong enough to survive it.

Each tiny moment of trust is a rebellion against the fear that tried to cage you. Each breath you take, unguarded, is a declaration: I am still here. And I am choosing life.

Joy Is Your Birthright

You do not have to earn your right to joy. You do not have to work for it, beg for it, or prove yourself worthy. Joy belongs to you simply because you exist because you survived the fire. Because you kept breathing when it felt impossible. Because your heart, though battered and bruised, kept beating to the rhythm of hope.

And now joy is ready to pour itself into you. Not the cautious, careful joy of someone afraid to be hurt. But the reckless, wholehearted, throw-your-head-back-and-laugh kind of joy. The kind where you lose yourself in a song. The kind where you make plans just because they excite you. The kind where you allow love, all forms of it, to pour into the cracks you once thought were fatal.

You are allowed to dance barefoot in your living room. You are allowed to book the trip without a second thought. You are allowed to fall madly, deeply, foolishly in love with life again. Joy is not a reward for healing. It is the oxygen of your new existence. Breathe it in, darling. Breathe it in.

The Legacy of Your Healing

You did not just heal for yourself. You healed for your daughters, so they know they never have to shrink to be loved. You healed for your sons, so they understand that real men honor the sacredness of a woman's heart. You healed for your future, for the grandchildren you will hold, for the generations who will look at your life and see hope stitched into every scar.

Your healing echoes. It ripples across time. Every time you smile again, you dismantle the lie that pain has the final word. Every time you forgive yourself for being human, you tear down the fortress of shame that trapped so many before you. Every time you say *"I am worthy"*, you rewrite the story that generations tried to pass down.

You are a revolution wrapped in soft skin. You are a lighthouse standing tall against the storms. Your healing is a legacy, one of light, of love, of unstoppable grace.

And the world will be different because you were brave enough to choose yourself.

What Thriving Looks Like

It isn't neat. It isn't perfect. It's messy and magical and maddening and miraculous all at once. Thriving looks like:

- Making mistakes and laughing instead of punishing yourself.

- Crying on a random Tuesday and knowing it's not the end, just a moment.

- Loving so deeply and fiercely that everything around you blooms in your presence.

- Trust yourself, your gut, your heart, and your sacred knowing as you trust the ground beneath your feet..

- Waking up one morning and realizing: I am happy. And I did this. I built this life with my own blood, tears, and hope.

Thriving is the sound of your own laughter echoing through rooms once filled with silence. Thriving is the smell of your favorite coffee brewing as you plan a future you actually believe in. Thriving is the ability to rest, to love, to exist without apology.

You are not fragile anymore, my love. You are a wildfire. You are unstoppable. You are free.

The Celebration You Deserve

There is no expiration date on celebration. You don't have to wait until everything is perfect to throw a party for your soul. You are already enough. You have already won.

Celebrate the woman who:

- Refused to stay broken.
- Chose to heal, even when it hurt more than staying wounded.
- Created a life out of ruins and built a cathedral from the ashes.

Celebrate by:

- Buying yourself the flowers.
- Writing yourself love letters.
- Taking yourself out for a day of pure joy, no explanation needed.
- Looking in the mirror and saying, without hesitation: *"You are incredible, and I love you."*

You are the miracle you've been waiting for. You are the hope you once whispered for at 3 a.m. You are the proof that even shattered hearts can become masterpieces.

The Awkward Art of Becoming

Let's be honest, no one talks enough about the awkwardness of healing. Like, yes, you're thriving now... but also sometimes you're crying in the Target parking lot because a damn Hallmark commercial ambushed your emotional nervous system. You're out here building a new life one brave step at a time, but some days you still feel like you're walking barefoot over shattered glass while holding a latte and trying not to spill your soul.

Thriving doesn't mean polished. It means present. It means you show up to life in all your holy mess. Mascara smudged? Check. Boundaries up? Double check. Middle finger ready for anyone who tries to dim your light again? Oh, honey, you already know.

You've earned the right to be loud about your joy, unhinged in your laughter, and soft with yourself on the days it still hurts. That's what real thriving looks like, not some Pinterest-perfect version of healing, but a raw, radiant reclamation of everything they tried to take from you.

So yeah, maybe you still flinch when someone gets too close. Maybe you overanalyze texts or second-guess your own instincts. But you don't abandon yourself anymore. You don't shrink to make anyone comfortable. You are fiercely loyal to your heart, your truth, and your sacred boundaries.

And THAT is the kind of thriving no one can touch.

Closing Whispers

You made it. Not just through the heartbreak. Not just through the grief. You made it through you. Through every moment, you wanted to give up. Through every night, you thought the pain would eat you whole. Through every whispered lie that said you'd never feel whole again. But here you are. Radiant. Resurrected. Raw. Real. No longer shrinking, no longer settling, no longer sorry.

So, whisper this to your soul: I am not what they did to me. I am not the pain I carried. I am not the past that tried to define me.

I am the woman who rose. Who danced barefoot on her broken pieces and transformed them into stained glass windows. Who made her healing sacred. Who made her life a living altar. Who laughed again. Loved again. And lived again.

Welcome to your new life. You didn't just survive, you bloomed. And it looks breathtaking on you.

Soul Reflections

Questions to Sink Into

What does joy look like for me, not the version I was told I should want, but the version that sets my soul on fire?

_____
_____
_____
_____
_____
_____
_____

Where in my life am I still playing small, and what would it look like to unapologetically take up space there?

_____
_____
_____
_____

_____

_____

What would I do differently if I believed, without a doubt, that I am already enough?

_____

_____

_____

_____

_____

_____

In what ways can I celebrate myself, not someday, not later, but right now?

_____

_____

_____

_____

_____

_____

What does *"thriving"* mean in this season of my life... and am I brave enough to claim it?

_____

_____

_____

_____

_____

_____

Sacred Mantra

(Whisper it. Scream it. Tattoo it on your heart.)

"I am not waiting to be chosen, I choose myself, every damn day."

Healing Ritual: "The Radiance Ceremony"

What You'll Need:

- A gold or white candle

- A small glass of sparkling water or champagne

- A mirror

- A playlist that makes you feel unstoppable

- Your favorite outfit or robe

Step 1: Get Dressed Like You're the Celebration

Put on something that makes you feel electric. This is not the time for your *"meh"* sweatpants. You're about to honor your rebirth.

Step 2: Light the Candle

As you light it, say: *"This flame is my fire. My joy. My light. I am no longer afraid to shine."*

Step 3: Look in the Mirror and Toast Yourself

Hold the glass and look yourself in the eyes.

Say: *"To the woman who rose. Who healed. Who now thrives. I see you. I honor you. I celebrate you."*

Step 4: Sip, Sway, and Surrender

Play your anthem. Dance. Smile. Cry if you need to. Let your body feel the joy it's been denied for too long. You are the moment.

Step 5: Blow out the candle

Whisper: *"I am free. I am whole. I am home."*

Chapter 21:

Closing Message:

A Love Letter to Your Soul

Dear Beautiful Human, Soul Warrior

Look at you. Still here. Still breathing. Still trying. Still rising.

First, let me just say this: I am so freaking proud of you. Whether you crawled your way through this book, sobbed through it, side-eyed it with suspicion, or threw it across the room and came back later… thank you for showing up. You showed up for you. That's sacred. That's brave. That's badass.

This isn't just a closing chapter. This is me standing in front of you, heart wide open, arms stretched out, offering you the biggest, most soul-squeezing hug. This is me whispering in your ear, *"You did it."* And not because it's over, but because you made it through the part you thought would kill you.

Whether you chose to forgive and stay, or forgive and walk away, I honor you. Both choices take guts. Both take grace. Both are holy. One is not more noble than the other. You didn't need to prove your worth by enduring more pain. You didn't need to burn it all down to prove you're strong. You simply needed to choose what was true for you. And you did. Or maybe you're still figuring that out. That's okay too.

Let me remind you of something: There is no perfect path to healing. There's just your path. Sometimes it looks like yoga and green smoothies. Sometimes it looks like crying in your car with a

McFlurry in your lap. Sometimes it's blocking them. Sometimes it's having one last, honest conversation. Sometimes it's dancing like a lunatic in your kitchen to '90s R&B. Sometimes it's saying, *"I love you, but I love me more."* All of it counts. All of it heals.

You cracked open parts of yourself that you spent years trying to seal shut. You faced truths you didn't want to admit out loud. You held your own hand through nights that felt like forever. You laid boundaries like bricks, one painful decision at a time. You gave yourself permission to want more, and damn, that's not small.

To the one who stayed, I see you. I know how hard it is to rebuild trust when your heart still flinches at shadows. You chose to stay not because it was easy, but because you saw something worth saving. You stayed, and in staying, you demanded better, not just from them, but from yourself. You are not weak for staying. You are fierce for choosing love with your eyes wide open.

To the one who left, I see you too. I know the ache of walking away from a life you prayed would work out. You chose your peace over your pattern. You walked through the fire of grief and said, *"No more."* That takes courage. That takes soul. You didn't give up; you woke up. And in walking away, you chose to believe there's something more for you. And there is. So much more.

To the one still in the messy middle, you're not lost. You're becoming. Give yourself grace. Give yourself time. Don't rush the blooming. You're not late. You're just ripening.

This journey wasn't about fixing you. You were never broken. This was about remembering who you were before life told you to shrink. It was about reclaiming your voice, your power, your softness, your fire. It was about forgiving yourself for what you didn't know and loving yourself enough to never unlearn what you know now.

You are allowed to rewrite the ending. You are allowed to heal loudly or quietly. You are allowed to take up space in your own damn life. You are allowed to be both divine and a disaster some days. I mean it... cry in the shower, cuss in traffic, pray over coffee, text your therapist, light a candle, twerk in your underwear. All of it belongs. All of it is sacred.

You are the proof that survival can become art. That pain can birth power. That heartbreak can awaken hope. You are the hero of your own story. The love story with yourself? That's the main plot. Everything else is just side characters and plot twists.

So, here's my final offering to you: Keep your heart soft, but your standards high. Take no shit, but hold compassion. Laugh loudly. Love deeply. Heal audaciously. Rest when you're tired. Rise when you're ready. And for the love of all that is holy... never, ever forget who the hell you are.

You are magic. You are medicine. You are the afterglow of every storm you survived. I see you. I honor you. I celebrate you. I love you.

Always whispering, always cheering

Your Soul Whisperer

Acknowledgments

A love letter to the ones who made this book possible. To the souls who held me up. To the woman I used to be. And to my daughters... always, always to you.

To the ones who wept on floors no one saw... who screamed into pillows and danced in kitchens... who shattered and kept showing up anyway, this is for you. You are the heartbeat behind every page. You are the reason these words found life. Thank you for trusting me to whisper to the most sacred, silent parts of you.

To every woman who picked up this book with trembling hands and a heavy heart but still dared to hope, you are a warrior cloaked in grace. Whether you chose to forgive and stay, or forgive and walk away, or you're still standing in the messy middle trying to breathe, I honor you. I praise your courage. I celebrate your truth.

Thank you for letting me walk beside you. For letting me speak into your dark. For letting me remind you that healing doesn't have to look perfect, it just has to feel honest.

To the version of me who wasn't sure she would survive... I love you. I see you. Thank you for holding on. You fought for this story, and in doing so, you made room for everyone else to find their way, too.

To the ones who never left my circle, my soul tribe... thank you. Your presence was medicine. Your belief was balm. You listened without fixing, held space without judgment, and reminded me who I was when I almost forgot.

To the sacred earth, the wild ocean, and every tree that stood witness while I cracked open under the weight of becoming, thank you for holding me when nothing else could. You sang to my soul in the ancient tongue of wind and water and reminded me: I belong.

To my animals… my dogs, my cat, my cows, goats, pigs, chickens, and tortoises, thank you for showing me the purest form of love. You grounded me when the world spun too fast. You loved me without condition. You reminded me what it means to simply be.

And to my daughters… You are the truest, brightest light I've ever known. I watch you navigate this world with your own fire, your own strength, your own magic, and I am in awe. Thank you for loving me through my healing. Thank you for laughing with me when I wanted to cry, for hugging me when words fell short, and for teaching me what unconditional love really looks like. I am endlessly proud of the women you are becoming. I love you deeper than words will ever touch. You are the sacred why behind everything I do.

And finally… to you, dear reader. Whether we ever meet or only cross paths in these pages, know this: I see you. I believe in you. I celebrate the hell out of you.

May this book be your mirror, your sanctuary, your spark. May it remind you in the deepest way that you were never broken. You were becoming. You are the miracle. You are the masterpiece. You are the story the world so desperately needs.

With endless gratitude, with reverence, and with so much love,

Your Soul Whisperer

www.ingramcontent.com/pod-product-compliance
Lightning Source LLC
Chambersburg PA
CBHW051902090426
42811CB00003B/437